BIBLE STUDY COMMENTARY

Ephesians - 2 Thessalonians

Bible Study Commentary

Ephesians– 2 Thessalonians

IAN CUNDY

ARK PUBLISHING
130 City Road, London EC1V 2NJ

CHRISTIAN LITERATURE CRUSADE
Fort Washington, Pennsylvania 19034

©1981 Ark Publishing (UK dist.)
130 City Road, London EC1V 2NJ

Christian Literature Crusade (USA dist.)
Box C, Ft. Washington, PA 19034

First published 1981

ISBN 0 86201 086 1 (UK)
ISBN 0 87508 173 8 (USA)

Maps: Jenny Grayston

Phototypeset in Great Britain by
Filmtype Services Limited, Scarborough
Printed in U.S.A.

General Introduction

The worldwide church in the last quarter of the twentieth century faces a number of challenges. In some places the church is growing rapidly and the pressing need is for an adequately trained leadership. Some Christians face persecution and need support and encouragement while others struggle with the inroads of apathy and secularism. We must come to terms, too, with the challenges presented by Marxism, Humanism, a belief that 'science' can conquer all the ills of mankind, and a whole range of Eastern religions and modern sects. If we are to make anything of this confused and confusing world it demands a faith which is solidly biblical.

Individual Christians, too, in their personal lives face a whole range of different needs – emotional, physical, psychological, mental. As we think more and more about our relationships with one another in the body of Christ and as we explore our various ministries in that body, as we discover new dimensions in worship and as we work at what it means to embody Christ in a fallen world we need a solid base. And that base can only come through a relationship with Jesus Christ which is firmly founded on biblical truth.

The Bible, however, is not a magical book. It is not enough to say, 'I believe', and quote a few texts selected at random. We must be prepared to work with the text until our whole outlook is moulded by it. We must be ready to question our existing position and ask the true meaning of the word for us in our situation. All this demands careful study not only of the text but also of its background and of our culture. Above all it demands prayerful and expectant looking to the Spirit of God to bring the word home creatively to our own hearts and lives.

This new series of books has been commissioned in response to the repeated requests for something new to follow on from Bible Characters and Doctrines. It is now over ten years since the first series of Bible Study Books were produced and it is hoped they will reflect the changes of the last ten years and bring the Bible text to life for a new generation of readers. The series has three aims:

1. To encourage regular, systematic personal Bible reading. Each volume is divided into sections ideally suited to daily use, and will normally provide material for three months (the exceptions being Psalms and 1 Corinthians-Galatians, four months, and Mark and Ezra-Job, two months). Used in this way the books will cover the entire Bible in five years. The comments aim to give background information and enlarge on the meaning of the text, with special reference to the contemporary relevance. Detailed questions of application are, however, often left to the reader. The questions for further study are designed to aid in this respect.

2. To provide a resource manual for group study. These books do not provide a detailed plan for week by week study. Nor do they present a group leader with a complete set of ready-made questions or activity ideas. They do, however, provide the basic biblical material and, in the questions for further discussion, they give starting points for group discussion

3. To build into a complete Bible commentary. There is, of course, no shortage of commentaries. Here, however, we have a difference. Rather than look at the text verse by verse the writers examine larger blocks of text, preserving the natural flow of the original thought and observing natural breaks.

Writers have based their comments on the RSV and some have also used the New International Version in some detail. The books can, however, be used with any version.

Introduction

Since the time of the early church the epistle to the Ephesians has been a source of debate. The phrase 'in Ephesus' (1:1) is omitted by some of the earliest manuscripts we possess as well as by Origen writing at the beginning of the third century. Add to that the apparent absence of any specific situation, the close similarity with Colossians, especially the common reference to Tychicus (Eph. 6:21 and Col. 4:7), and the reference to a letter to (or from) Laodicea in Colossians 4:16 and you have plenty of scope for a detective novel. As early as Marcion, a second-century heretic, it was suggested that this was the letter to Laodicea. More recently others have doubted its Pauline authorship (for a fuller discussion see Francis Foulkes, *Ephesians,* an Introduction and Commentary, Tyndale Press 1963, pp. 13–40).

It seems probable that both Ephesians and Colossians were written about the same time by Paul, imprisoned in Rome, though J. A. T. Robinson has recently suggested they were written in Caesarea during the imprisonment described in Acts 24:22-27. (See *Re-dating the New Testament,* SCM, and *Can we trust the New Testament?* Mowbray.)

Structure
Comparison with Colossians shows not only a similar structure of doctrine, followed by associated exhortations and practical instruction, but also exposes some interesting insights into Paul's mind. The thoughts contained in the two prayers in Ephesians 1:15-19 and 3:14-21 are summed up in one prayer in Colossians 1:9-12. This, together with the broken sentence of 3:1, suggests that Paul is so carried away with the themes of his prayer that he gets diverted not once, but twice; first, into an elaboration of the glorious truth that the Ephesians are part of the people of God and their inheritance (1:15–2:22) and secondly, by the thought of his own ministry and God's grace in entrusting the gospel to him (3:2-21). It conjures up a delightful picture – human and full of encouragement – of the apostle so carried away by the marvellous themes he is handling that he forgets his orderly arrangement and structure.

Before embarking on a detailed study of the letter, you may find it helpful to read it straight through, making your own analysis of its major themes and argument.

Ephesians: Contents

1:1,2 Paul's credentials and greeting

Elsewhere (Galatians 1:1) Paul defends his claim to use the title 'apostle' – a word which means 'one who is sent'. The term has both a restricted and a wider use in the New Testament. More narrowly it refers to those who were the earthly disciples of Jesus and witnesses to his resurrection (Acts 1:21,22); Paul felt that his experience and commission on the road to Damascus met this requirement (Gal. 1:16; 1 Cor. 15:8-10). Its wider use embraces all who we today would describe as 'missionaries'. Paul's commission was to be sent by Jesus Christ to the Gentiles – a commission which was no accident, but given by divine command.

The recipients of the letter are described as 'saints' and also as 'faithful'. The NEB successfully removes some possible areas of mis-understanding by describing them as 'God's people' and 'believers'. The 'saints' in the New Testament are not a class of the especially holy or good, but simply those 'set apart' for God. The words 'at Ephesus' (NEB) are omitted by many early manuscripts, leading most scholars to suggest that they were added by someone who failed to see the character of the letter as a circular letter to the churches in Asia, intended for all God's people, for all believers in Jesus Christ (1).

Paul's greeting, although a customary one with him, introduces the readers to two central themes to which he will return later – the grace of God (see chs. 1–3) and the peace of Christ (see 2:14).

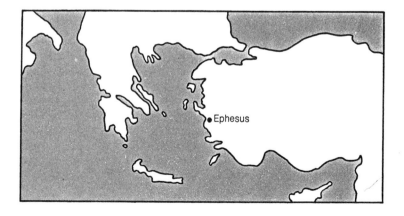

1:3-14 A 'planned' people

One of Paul's favourite descriptions of a Christian is 'in Christ' – note the repeated 'in him' in verses 3,4,6,7,9,10,11,13. Here he lists some of the privileges of belonging to this corporate personality as an act of praise to God for all the resources that we possess, for we are not lacking in any spiritual blessing (3).

These verses embrace all the great themes of the Christian gospel: God's call (4) and redemption in Christ to create a new united kingdom of Christ (7,9,10); the responsibility that is laid on those who believe and 'hoped in Christ' 'to live for the praise of his glory' (12) and finally the gift that makes it all possible and assures us that it is true, the Holy Spirit. All this is the expression of 'the riches of his grace'.

Paul's first thought is the fact of God's eternal purpose (4-6). We are a planned people, a people with a purpose (4), a people of privilege (5). The so-called doctrine of election is one that has disturbed many people. If God chose us 'before the foundation of the world', does that leave any room for human response and freedom? Rightly understood, however, it is 'full of sweet, pleasant, and unspeakable comfort to godly persons' as the Book of Common Prayer quaintly puts it. Here Paul uses the doctrine to assure us that our status is *(a)* part of God's eternal plan – 'he marked us out beforehand' and *(b)* rests not on our fallible initiative, but on his unchanging purpose. To deny this is to make God capricious and our salvation as uncertain and insecure as our fickle human promises.

THOUGHT: We are a planned people, a people with a purpose, a people of privilege.

1:3-14 Bound together by the Holy Spirit

The second important theme of Paul's thinking which is in this opening 'hymn' of praise is the corporate nature of the gospel.

Of course all the blessings described by Paul are mine as an individual believer in Christ, but I am never alone in enjoying them; they are 'ours' – 'God has blessed *us*'; '*we* have redemption'; his plan is to *unite* all things. John Donne, meditating on the funeral bell as he lay on his sick-bed, penned the justly famous words already quoted: 'No man is an island, entire of itself; every man is a piece of the continent, a part of the main: if a clod be washed away by the sea, Europe is the less, as well as if a promontory were; . . . any man's death diminishes me, because I am involved in mankind; And therefore never send to know for whom the bell tolls; It tolls for thee.' John Donne was writing to every man. The insight is, however, even more applicable to every Christian. By his incorporation into Christ – by being, in Paul's words, 'in Christ' – he is part of the whole. Just as Father, Son and Holy Spirit belong together and work for a common divine purpose, as this passage demonstrates (see 3,5,9,10,13,14), so those in Christ belong to the 'one new man' (2:15) – the single new humanity of Christ with one purpose (12).

A third theme is the crucial role of the Holy Spirit: he is the seal and the guarantee that all these blessings really do apply to us (13,14). The word guarantee (Gk. *arrabōn*) is a lovely word to be applied to the Holy Spirit. In the time of the New Testament it meant a 'down payment' or pledge which guaranteed the full payment to come. In modern Greek it is used of an engagement ring. Paul uses it three times to describe the Holy Spirit (2 Cor. 1:21,22; 2 Cor. 5:5; Eph. 1:14). The context in Corinthians is subtly different to that in Ephesians. Here the fact that God's Spirit comes to be in us guarantees our inheritance – the full benefits of our redemption – while in 2 Corinthians Paul uses the same thought to assure his readers that God's promises really apply to them and that they will one day enjoy the benefits of the resurrection body.

THOUGHT: Here is the basic ground of Christian assurance: God through his Holy Spirit has come to live his life in us.

Additional note on corporate solidarity and corporate personality

To Western minds the idea that we can be bound up in the actions of another person may seem strange. We inherit a tradition which places a stronger emphasis on individual action and individual responsibility – I am responsible for my own actions and must suffer the consequences on my own. To the Hebrew mind that was short-sighted. He was more conscious of the fact that he was inseparably linked to others and that one man's action could affect the whole nation.

On the physical level this is one reason for the continuing coherence of the Jewish people during the centuries when they had no recognised homeland. In terms of our understanding of the New Testament it lies behind Paul's doctrine of the atonement: how Christ's death affects me; of being a Christian – being 'in Christ'; and of the Church.

We tend to stress the judicial model of the atonement – he died in my place and paid the penalty instead of me. Paul certainly uses that picture (e.g. Ephesians 1:7 – though even there his favourite phrase 'in Christ' creeps in), but the idea of our sharing and being involved in Christ's death and resurrection is perhaps more crucial to his argument in Ephesians and Colossians. We were involved in these actions (Colossians 2:9-12 – in verses 13,14 another picture of 'cancelling the debt' is added [compare 2:20; 3:1-4] we died and now live so that 'Christ is our life', see also Ephesians 2:14-16).

Paul extends this idea to his understanding of being a Christian – we are part of this corporate personality; we are 'in Christ'. The Israelites learnt the bitter consequences of such corporate responsibility at Ai (Joshua 7). Although only one man had looted the town, 'the Israelites defied the ban', Achan's sin became, or *was*, the sin of Israel as a body.

As Christians we are part of the corporate personality of the body of Christ – a 'new humanity', 'fellow-citizens with God's people' – we are bound up in Christ and with each other.

This understanding, so important to Paul, has far-reaching consequences for Christian thinking and living. We cannot be Christians 'on our own', for to be a Christian is to be part of this corporate entity – the body of Christ. We are certainly responsible for our own actions, but not exclusively so – our behaviour, good or bad, affects the body and we have a mutual responsibility for each other.

We hear a lot today from secular sociologists and others about 'the need for community'. It is there in the gospel! Here is the real community in which we are bound in Christ so that, as Paul reminds us in 1 Corinthians 12, if one member suffers we all suffer; if one rejoices we all rejoice – including Christ, the head of the body. That is the intimacy and the responsibility of living 'in union with Christ'.

John Donne, meditating from his sick-bed on the funeral bell, expressed it so well:

Perchance he for whom this Bell tolls, may be so ill, as that he knows not it tolls for him; and perchance I may think myself so much better than I am, as that they who are about me, and see my state, may have caused it to toll for me, and I know not that. The Church is catholic, universal, so are all her actions; all that she does belongs to all. When she baptises a child, that action concerns me; for that child is thereby connected to that Head which is my Head too, and engraffed into that body, whereof I am a member. And when she buries a man, that action concerns me. . . . The Bell doth toll for him that thinks it doth . . . Who bends not his ear to any bell which upon any occasion rings? But who can remove it from that bell, which is passing a piece of himself out of this world? No man is an island, entire of itself; every man is a piece of the continent, a part of the main; if a clod be washed away by the sea, Europe is the less, as well as if a promontory were; any man's death diminishes me, because I am involved in mankind. And therefore never send to know for whom the bell tolls; it tolls for thee.

1:15-23 Christ-centred prayer

As Paul begins to pray for the Christians in Ephesus and the surrounding churches his thoughts are still dominated by Jesus Christ and what he has achieved. His conviction of the centrality of Christ for Christian life and growth arises straight out of his own experience. This conviction appears in three ways in these verses.

First, the heart of his prayer is that they may deepen their faith through a greater knowledge of God (17), a knowledge gained through Christ's work and words. If we are to grow as Christians this must be our first concern, we must deepen our knowledge, that is, our personal experience of God and our relationship with him, the Father, Son and Holy Spirit. If we read these verses with Paul's prayer in 3:14-21 the Trinitarian reference is clear. Our knowledge of God is knowledge of the Father (1:17), his achievements in Christ (1:19,20), and the strengthening presence of God's Spirit through whom Christ 'dwells in our hearts' (3:17) and we are filled with 'all the fullness of God' (3:19).

Secondly, his vision is of the 'cosmic Christ'. The full power of God is to be seen in the resurrection of Christ and in his present universal authority. Paul stresses this by using four synonyms (19) – power (*dunamis*); working (*energeia*, compare energy in English); strength (*kratos*); and might (*ischus*). It is this picture of Christ as Lord over all which fires Paul's prayer and his theology.

Thirdly, and with most audacity, Paul asserts that this universal Christ expresses himself through the church, his body (22,23). Paul uses the idea of the church as a body in two ways. In Romans 12:3-8 and 1 Corinthians 12:12-27 it is simply an analogy of how the church works, like a body with mutually dependent members. Here, however, and in Colossians, he develops this thought by referring to the church specifically as the body *of Christ*. Just as my body is the means through which I express my thoughts and feelings, so the risen and exalted Lord expresses himself in the world today through his body, the church.

The closing verse of the chapter emphasises this point. It is notoriously difficult to render its precise meaning in English (compare NEB). Professor C. F. D. Moule has helpfully isolated four possible interpretations (*Colossians and Philemon*, CUP, 1958, p. 167f) though he himself admits to suspending 'judgement over the difficult Eph. 1:22,23'! Having said that, he concludes that the word 'fullness' (*plērōma*) in Ephesians and Colossians suggests 'that Christ is thought of as containing, representing, all that God is; and that the destiny of Christians, as the Body of Christ, is to enter, in him, into that wealth and completeness' (p. 169). That is, of course, a corporate destiny – we, as a church, a community, are to express the fullness of God.

2:1-7 From death to life

Paul is often accused of writing complicated sentences! These verses are no exception. In the Greek the main verb – 'made alive' – is in verse 5, but most English translations break the sentence up by putting a verb in the first verse. Paul, carried away with the thought of the amazing power of God which was seen in the resurrection and exaltation, points out that Jew and Gentile – is the change from 'us' to 'you' in 1:13 significant? – are both made alive by grace. We (Jews) were part of God's eternal plan, but you also (Gentiles) believed and received the Spirit so that we (Jew and Gentile) are both his workmanship (2:10), both made alive by God (2:5).

This sentence (2:1-7) begins with the object 'you, who were . . ., God made alive . . .', but as it unravels everybody, Jew and Gentile alike, are included in its assertion of sinfulness (3). The thrice repeated 'following' (2,3, RSV), although translating two different Greek words, reminds us that the man without Christ is actively pursuing a course based on self-interest and the way of the world. In contrast the Christian is 'made alive together with Christ' and God, not man, is now the initiator.

Paul's language in verses 1-3 is very strong, even to the point of describing the non-Christian state as 'death' (1). Such language is obviously analogous – after all, a dead man cannot walk (2)! Even so it poses a problem for many people, even though some may find it only too appropriate, for sin has killed their innocence, ideals and will (William Barclay). However, we all have non-Christian friends who may appear to lead more 'Christian' lives than we and whose standards are the same as our own. Two things need to be said. First, God's ethical standards are consistent with secure human existence. It should not surprise us, therefore, if people of other faiths, or of no faith, who are indeed made in the image of God, have perceived that life is best lived within an ethical framework. In a country whose laws have been shaped by Christian truth we should expect that to be doubly true. Secondly, Paul is here making a theological comment. In terms of a relationship to God, we are spiritually dead without Christ. It is only because of what God has done in and through Christ that a relationship with him can exist and 'live'. It is the divine 'but' of verse 4 that makes it all possible.

The idea of wealth or abundance – 'rich' and 'riches' (4,7; compare 1:7) – is once again in the front of Paul's mind. God out of the abundance of his mercy wishes to show the wealth of his grace to us. In these opening verses of Paul's letter the list of God's blessings is overwhelming. No wonder, therefore, that Paul exhausts his store of words for wealth, generosity and kindness.

2:8-10 Grace and workmanship

'Paul closes this passage', writes William Barclay, 'with one of the great expositions of the paradox which always lies at the heart of the Pauline view of the gospel.' We are saved 'not because of works'; we are 'created in Christ Jesus for good works'.

The first half of the paradox repeats the parenthesis of verse 5 and stresses *God's initiative* in salvation. We cannot earn our salvation for it is a gift of God's grace; we must simply accept it by faith. It is precisely at this point that the Christian gospel challenged the legalism of contemporary Judaism and still challenges the world's idea of what is 'fair'. The world apart from Christ rarely grasps the idea of grace. Like the labourers hired to work in the vineyard (Matthew 20:1-16) people today feel that those who do most should receive most. The gospel begins with the fact that none of us deserves salvation (compare 2:1-3); rather God grants it as a free and undeserved gift.

Some have followed this line of thought even further and suggested that 'the gift' of verse 8 refers to faith, so that no one can claim their belief as a kind of work which earns salvation – 'because I have faith, I am saved'. This understanding is not required by the Greek syntax and probably narrows Paul's thought unnecessarily. It is salvation by grace and through faith which is God's gift. Neither can it be contingent on faith, for faith is a responsive attitude. In response to God's overwhelming love I must simply accept; that is a humbling activity and can never be a cause for boasting. Sadly, even at this point our arrogance can creep in. To say, for example, 'I made a decision for Jesus Christ' may describe a remembered experience, but it is dangerously near the boasting Paul rightly condemns. None of us likes the humbling experience of the gospel –

> *Nothing in my hand I bring,*
> *Simply to thy cross I cling:*
> *Naked, come to thee for dress;*
> *Helpless, look to thee for grace . . .*

The second arm of the paradox emphasises the implications of salvation. 'All the good works in the world cannot put us right with God; but once we have been put right with God there is something radically wrong with the Christianity which does not issue in good works' (Wilbarclay). Paul picks up the thought of 1:4,12 and stresses our divinely prepared role. The word he uses for 'workmanship' (10) is elsewhere only found in Romans 1:20. In that passage it refers to the works of God's creation, here to his re-creation.

Questions for further study and discussion on Ephesians 1:1–2:10

1. Paul lists a number of 'spiritual blessings' in these verses. How would you describe these to people today who do not understand, as Paul's readers did, terms like 'redemption', 'salvation', etc? What is the purpose of these blessings (1:4-6,12)?

2. What do you find most comforting and most challenging in 1:2-14?

3. What would you say are the three dominant characteristics of society today? If people really saw the power and glory of the exalted Christ and the riches of heaven, in what ways would these characteristics change?

4. Your group or your church is a hand or leg of the world-wide body of Christ, sharing in his fullness (1:23). In what practical ways do you or could you express this?

5. Sheer outgoing generous love is at the centre of life and 'In response to God's overwhelming love, I must simply accept' (page 16). The belief in unearned mercy and salvation is alien to the spirit of the world and of every other religion. In what ways should our response be evident? Are there any ways in which we act as though we don't really believe in it?

6. We are supposed to do only those good works which God has planned for us to do (2:10). In what ways is this verse encouraging and challenging?

7. 'We are his workmanship' (2:10). What factors within our group tend to destroy God's work? Make this a subject of prayer.

2:11-13 A barrier abolished

Paul now turns from a general exposition of the blessings of salvation to a particular problem which troubled the early church: the division of Jews and Gentiles. Elsewhere in his letter (3:1-10) he emphasises his unique role as the apostle to the Gentiles, to some of whom he is writing. So he reminds his readers of the Jewish view of their former status.

To us today it seems strange that the barrier could be so absolute: Jews believing that Gentiles were 'fuel for the fires of hell', condemning them because they did not bear the covenant sign of circumcision. Israel should have shared their faith with other nations (compare Gen. 12:3; Isa. 42:1,6), but because their thinking was superficial ('in the flesh') the Jews had failed to perceive the true meaning of this sign. In other letters Paul is at pains to point out the spiritual reality which contrasted with the physical sign (1 Cor. 7:19; Gal. 5:6; 6:15; Col. 2:11; Rom. 2:25-29). Here he expounds the privileges which they failed to enjoy before Christ came: they were strangers to the community of Israel and outside the covenants of promise which God made to Abraham (Gen. 12:2,3; 13:14-17; 15:1; 17:1,2) and repeated to Isaac and Jacob. The result was hopelessness and Godlessness.

Once again the divine 'but' (13) means that all has changed. Those whom the Rabbis described as far from the privileges of the covenant people were now brought near in Christ. In saying this Paul is not only pointing out that the Jewish/Gentile barrier is demolished in the Christian church but, by implication, that Christ has fulfilled the Old Testament promises. This theme is not expounded here, but is central to his argument in Romans and Galatians. When a Jew acknowledges that fulfilment he does not cease to be a Jew but recognises in Jesus the Christ, the Messiah, he has been waiting for. Christian Jew and Christian Gentile therefore now together inherit the covenant promise: together they belong to the 'new Israel' – the church of God; they share a common hope and know the same God.

CHALLENGE: Today we may not be so conscious that we are 'Gentiles', though the unity of the gospel is still desperately needed in the Middle East. However, the principles behind Paul's thought apply to many similar divisions in our modern world. It is all too easy to imply, often unconsciously, that barriers of race, colour or culture exclude people from our Christian heritage. In Christ no one is 'far off', we are all 'brought near in his blood'.

2:14-18 The end of barriers

One of Isaiah's great visions is of God turning aside his anger at Israel's sin and crying, 'Peace, peace, to the far and to the near' (Isa. 57:19). Isaiah probably meant the Jews in exile and those still in Palestine, but Paul, following the usage of the Rabbis, gives Isaiah's message a new significance. 'For he is our peace,' says Paul (14), the peace of the Gentiles who are far off (13) as well as of the Jews who are near (compare 17).

For Paul the division between Jew and Gentile was so absolute that he could speak of a 'dividing wall of hostility' (14). If the mortar of the wall was the enmity and hatred which characterised Jewish relations with Gentiles, then the bricks were the rules and regulations of Jewish ceremonial and religious law. It was through the observance of these ceremonies that the devout Jew sought to obtain salvation: they had the added effect of isolating him from his Gentile neighbour. Both bricks and mortar have gone! Through the life and death of the man of Nazareth – this is the significance of 'in his flesh' (15) – the barrier has been broken down. Although Paul is not expounding his understanding of either the Incarnation or the Atonement, it is significant that both are here – '*he came* and preached peace' (17), 'in his flesh' (15), 'through the cross' (16).

The result of this demolition is always seen in terms of a double reconciliation – to God and to our fellow-men. So Christ creates 'in himself, one new man' (15); he reconciles 'us both to God in one body' (16) and 'through him we both have access in one Spirit to the Father' (18). This link between our relationship to God and to each other runs throughout the New Testament, from Jesus' summary of the law – 'Love God with your whole being and your neighbour as yourself' – to John's ridicule of the man who claims to love God but hates his brother (1 John 4:20). The two are so closely entwined in the New Testament that one does not follow from the other; rather they belong together in the outworking of the gospel.

For Paul, therefore, in the act of becoming Christian, we become part of the 'single new humanity' (15, NEB). We are henceforth 'in Christ', part of his corporate personality in solidarity with him and all our fellow believers. And we cannot be reconciled to God without being part of the body. Too many Christians think that belonging to the church, the body of Christ, follows on as a second stage after a personal allegiance to Christ. The logic of Paul's phraseology is that this is a parody of the gospel. When we are in Christ we are in his body: Paul knows of no half-way house. Then we all equally have unimpeded access to the Father 'in the one Spirit' (18).

2:19-22 God's new building

The unity inherent in Christ leads Paul to develop three of his many images of the church. We have already noticed his use of the body (compare comment on 1:23) and the new humanity (2:15). Here we have the images of being fellow citizens, members of the same family (or household, RSV) and bricks in the temple of God. Each of these images emphasises the idea of belonging to a corporate entity in which the whole is greater than the sum of its parts. So, a building is not just a collection of stones or bricks. It is a total concept designed by the architect and erected by the builder. The family is not a random set of individuals but a close-knit group acting together, united by a bond of blood, bearing a family likeness. We are 'fellow citizens with the saints', those set apart in Christ. Again the word 'saints' is rarely, if ever, used in the singular in the New Testament – we are, together, 'the saints', God's own people.

The way Paul develops the analogy of the temple in these verses reminds us that structures are important although we rightly fear the dangers of institutionalisation – even the word is ugly! When Paul refers to the 'foundation of the apostles and prophets' (20) he does not mean that every church, local or national, should have apostles and prophets today, but that these men were 'the ascended Lord's foundation gifts to the church' (F. F. Bruce). We belong to the church of the apostles – the church of Peter, James and Paul. It is clear from writings like the Didache dating from the first century, that there were a number of itinerant ministers and prophets (who sometimes clashed with the more settled elders and deacons). These, too, says Paul, belong to the one temple. The picture in Paul's mind is therefore of the total church in which Christ occupies the key position (the cornerstone, v.20) but of which all, from the apostles onward, are a vital part. From our perspective the building embraces many more generations of Christian people than ever Paul imagined, but we all belong together in the structure.

Elsewhere, especially in 1 Corinthians, Paul points out the need for this united structure to be clearly visible. This is also true of his vision here. The quest for the right sort of historical continuity and visible unity within the church does not lead up a blind alley, but is a necessary expression of New Testament imagery. Such a quest has a missionary emphasis, for it is in this structure that God dwells (22) and through it that he is seen in the world – 'the living God displays his presence in the world through a living household created by the Holy Spirit' (W. L. Lane, *Ephesians–2 Thessalonians*, SU, 1969).

3:1-7 The mystery of Christ

We have already noted in the introduction the significance of the broken sentence in 3:1. The reason for Paul's prayer – the richness of God's love and grace expressed in all that Christ has done for the Gentiles – is given in chapters 1 and 2, but the prayer does not continue till verse 14. Verses 2-13 are a digression prompted by Paul's reference to his imprisonment (1).

Paul probably wrote this letter from prison in Rome (see introduction), while he was awaiting trial after he had escaped the Jews' anger by exercising his right of appeal to Caesar (Acts 25:11). Technically a prisoner of Emperor Nero, he describes himself as 'the prisoner of Christ Jesus' (1, NEB – a literal translation of the Greek). Perhaps as he wrote he remembered the Lord's words, 'you must bear witness also at Rome' (Acts 23:11); certainly he realised that he was in prison for the sake of Christ and his gospel and that it was because of his mission to the Gentiles that he suffered.

With a deliberate play on words, Paul describes his message as 'the mystery of Christ' (4, compare v.3). To the educated Greek the word mystery (*mustērion*), which Paul has already used in 1:9, would conjure up thoughts of the mystery religions, the secret cults open only to initiates. The Christian mystery which Paul defines in Col. 1:27 as 'Christ in you, the hope of glory', is no secret cult, but rather is open to Gentile as well as Jew. It is this aspect of the mystery of Christ that Paul is at pains to stress and so he sums up the argument of chapter 2 in one pithy sentence (6).

This mystery came *by revelation* (3). Describing his experience on the road to Damascus, Paul relates how it was to the Gentiles that God had sent him (Acts 26:17,18). God had spoken and his mission was plain. Even though it was contrary to all his Jewish prejudices he preached to them so that they might receive 'a place among those who are sanctified by faith in God'. This novel insight was not disclosed to former generations but declared to apostles and prophets by the Holy Spirit (5). Peter, for example, received a vision (Acts 10) and had to explain his actions to the other apostles; only the evident coming of the Holy Spirit on Cornelius and his household silenced their opposition. But it was still left to Paul to be the prime minister to the Gentiles – this was 'the stewardship [the assignment] of God's grace which was given to him' (2). Insights as fundamental to the gospel as this were the special prerogative of the apostolic age, but we should not preclude the possibility of God revealing things which were not disclosed to a previous generation; certainly we all have insights to share and tasks to perform for which we are uniquely qualified.

3:8-13 The church's task – and Paul's

It would be very easy to exalt oneself if one were entrusted, as Paul was, with the task of presenting the gospel to a completely new area and people. Yet all the great missionaries, from Paul to Hudson Taylor, have shared a self-effacing humility. For Paul it is expressed in two ways.

First, he describes himself as 'less than the least of all God's people' (8). He coins a comparative ('less') from a word that is already a superlative ('least') in order to stress the point. To us it seems false modesty at the very least, but that would be to miss the direction of Paul's thinking. His mind is occupied not so much by a comparison with others, but by a continuing amazement that the man who persecuted the church and never deserved God's mercy should be entrusted with this overwhelming commission. No wonder he finds the wealth of Christ 'unsearchable', that is, impossible to trace out with human feet – a word used by Job and his friends as they tried to fathom God's way (Job 5:9; 9:10).

Secondly, he realises that this task was assigned to him, not as an individual, but as a member of the church. If we take the 'in order that' which opens v.10 to refer back to the main verb, Paul's point is that he was given the double task of preaching to the Gentiles and of making all men see the plan of God, in order that *the church's* task might be achieved. His personal missionary calling merely focuses or enshrines the calling of the church. It is the responsibility of the church to make known 'the manifold wisdom of God'. Perhaps if we rediscovered this corporate sense of responsibility we should be able to place our individual gifts and responsibilities in perspective. We are not all evangelists, we are not all meant to be 'leading men to Christ' every moment of our lives, but the church has a continual duty to preach the gospel and present men mature in Christ. In that *corporate* task we all have a significant position, but it may be as a full-back rather than a centreforward!

The church's task is to make 'the "many-faceted" wisdom of God known to the principalities and powers in the heavenly places'. Paul stresses the spiritual nature of our task and the authority of the gospel over all spiritual or human powers. For the wisdom of God is many-faceted (*polupoikilos*) – it 'will match with any situation which life may bring to us' (William Barclay).

Seen in this wider, eternal perspective (11) Paul's imprisonment is a means of glory, not an occasion for sorrow and discouragement (compare Col. 1:24). A further reason for encouragement is the access we have to God himself through our faith in Christ (12).

3:14-19 Paul's earnest prayer

There is nothing half-hearted about Paul's renewed prayer. Not only is he moved to pray by his vision of the manifold grace and blessings of God – every time he begins his prayer (1:15; 3:1,14) he has added yet another reason for doing so – but he also kneels to pray, an expression of earnestness and concern.

Paul's prayer is essentially Trinitarian. His approach is to 'the Father' – the best manuscripts omit 'of our Lord Jesus Christ' (AV) – who is the pattern of all fatherhood. The phrase is more naturally translated as 'every family' rather than 'the whole family' as there is no definite article in the Greek. The thought is therefore that all relationships of fatherhood are based on the character of the Fatherhood of God, both in relation to the other persons of the Trinity and to the created order. We often use the analogy of God being like a human father. In terms of our comprehension, that is fair, but theologically the analogy works the other way. My fatherhood should be like that of God. That is an awesome responsibility.

The first request Paul makes for his readers is for spiritual strength (16; compare 1:19 and Col. 1:11), 'to be made capable by his power'. Once again such a request is to be met 'according to the riches of his glory' and appropriated by faith (17). The request is a double one – to be strengthened by the Spirit and to be inhabited by Christ – a couplet which stresses the unbreakable link between Christ and his Spirit. We are so loose in our use of language that we can easily imply an 'indwelling' by Christ separate from that of the Spirit. In Paul's thought they belong together for it is only through the Spirit that Christ can 'dwell in our hearts'. In God's dealings with us the persons of the Trinity are never divided.

The prime character of God's life in us is love. So Paul prays with a double metaphor that their foundations and roots may be those of love. (The variation in the NEB, which takes the phrase 'in love' with the first half of the verse is grammatically possible though perhaps less likely; see F. Foulkes, p. 103.) Then, *together*, 'with all the saints' (18), they will grasp the magnitude of God's love and understand the love of Christ. The thought may seem tortuous, but the apprehension of Christian truth is both corporate and practical – it is grasped through the practical outworking of love within the Christian community.

The goal of all this, to 'be filled with all the fullness of God', is no less startling (19; compare 1:23 and 4:13). As Professor Moule has it (see comment on 1:23), 'the fullness (of God or of Christ) is the condition, astonishingly, to which Christians are destined to be brought'.

3:20,21 God's infinite power

Paul has just asked that his readers might be 'filled with all the fullness of God' (19). Is it not, then, the height of hyperbole to conclude by offering an ascription 'to him who . . . is able to do far more abundantly than all that we ask or think' (20)? This is not mere hyperbole but the truth boldly stated. If Christ dwells in our hearts through his Holy Spirit; if the life and fullness of God fills us as members of the body of Christ, then he who is at work within us can perform acts which far outstrip our finite human conceptions. The sad fact is that most of us and most of our churches have failed to grasp the immeasurable resources which are at his and our disposal.

In his final ascription of praise Paul returns to the twin themes of these opening chapters: the task of the church and the blessings that are ours in and through Jesus Christ. So 'to him be glory in the church and in Christ Jesus'. Glory is to be offered in the church, for, as we have seen, the church is the means through which the character and personality of God are to be seen in his world. To the church is also entrusted the task of making Christ known. In both senses God must be glorified for the rest of time and beyond.

God's glory is also continually seen 'in Christ Jesus', for he 'has blessed us in Christ with every spiritual blessing in the heavenly places' (1:3). Thus as these blessings are seen the love of Christ and hence the glory of God are demonstrated. So Christ and his church are linked together as the means of bringing glory to God, in anticipation of the intimate relationship with which they are described in 5:21-27.

CHALLENGE: The sad fact is that most of us and most of our churches have failed to grasp the immeasurable resources which are at Christ's, and our, disposal.

Questions for further study and discussion on Ephesians 2:11–3:21

1. From the first three chapters, how would you sum up Paul's central theme and concern in writing? What are the key stages in his argument?

2. 'Having no hope and without God in the world' – what groups of people in society would you say these words most aptly describe? Is there anything you or your church could do for any of these groups?

3. Jesus 'has broken down the dividing wall of hostility' (2:14). What barriers are there in today's world? In what ways is the church working to destroy these hostile divisions?

4. 'Jesus is our peace.' What does that mean for you (2:14,15)?

5. What qualities of the church does Paul emphasise in 2:18-22? Who holds the church together? What is the church's purpose? How is it being achieved in your fellowship?

6. Paul was made an apostle to the Gentiles by the will of God (1:1; 3:1-8). We are all given specific tasks and gifts (compare 4:8-12; 1 Cor. 12). How can we know what these are?

7. Sometimes other people can see better than we can. Go round the group suggesting the strongest gifts of each member.

8. How is the inner man (the will, the conscience, the reason) to be strengthened (3:16)? How can we experience this in our everyday lives?

9. Love is a much abused word – how would you define and describe it (3:17-19)? How is it entered into? How is it experienced? We talk a lot about love, but many of us experience little of it; why would you say this is?

4:1 Worthy of our calling

The central argument of Ephesians is concerned with the resolution of the world's disunity in the new humanity of Christ. It is, says Paul, God's ultimate purpose that in Christ all barriers between men and nations should be torn down. It is the corporate calling of the Christian church to make that message known. So, having established his theme, Paul now turns to its implications. The phrase of verse 1 – 'I beg you to lead a life worthy of your calling' – is worked out in terms of the church and its ministry (4:1-16); the church and its inner life (4:17–5:21) and its family relationships – wives, husbands, children and slaves (5:22–6:9); with a final section (6:10-20) on the weapons with which we are equipped to fulfil our calling.

'The Church,' writes William Barclay, 'must be the body through which Christ acts and the voice through which he speaks. The Church must be Christ's instrument in bringing this divine unity into the world. But if the Church is to succeed in that great task, the people within the Church must be a certain kind of people' (*Letters to Galatians and Ephesians*, The Daily Study Bible, St. Andrew Press, 1972, p. 157).

Into this headline to the second section of his letter Paul slips an aside – 'a prisoner for the Lord' (1). He has already used a similar phrase in 3:1, but there is a subtle difference. In the Greek text, in the first phrase he writes of being 'a prisoner *of* Christ Jesus' while here he writes that he is 'a prisoner *in* the Lord'. The difference can obviously be overplayed, but on this occasion he is, perhaps, concerned not to arouse their sympathy or to point out that his chains are on their account; rather he wishes them to realise that his whole life is lived in captivity to Christ – he is truly a prisoner in the Lord. 'The chains of his imprisonment limited his bodily movement, but his life was most truly controlled by the fact that it was "in the Lord"' (F. Foulkes, *Ephesians*, IVP, 1963, p. 107).

4:1-6 The unity of the Spirit

It is important to grasp the logic of this chapter. Paul begins by asserting the oneness of the body of Christ (4-6). The gifts of its members, however, are different and varied (7-11), and this very diversity builds up the body, strengthens its unity, and brings maturity to its members (12-16). There is a circular pattern: an essential unity, and an active diversity which builds up the unity and makes united growth possible.

Before embarking on the first stage of this argument, Paul lists five qualities of the life 'worthy of the calling to which |we| have been called'. The first is 'lowliness' or humility. Significantly, the noun seems to have come into currency with the New Testament. The adjective appears previously in classical Greek in a derogatory sense, for humility was not a virtue to the Greeks. To Christians, however, it was the essential characteristic of Christ and of God (see comment on Phil. 2:5-11). The second is 'meekness', in the sense of gentleness of character. It is the quality of the man who has 'every instinct and every passion . . . under perfect control' (William Barclay). Patience comes next. The word means 'longsuffering', not in the sense of enduring pain but of slowness to react. It is an essential quality if community life is to have any hope of success. 'Forbearing one another in love' (2) is its outcome. Through a real Christian love the patient man is able to tolerate another's weakness – those faults and foibles which can be so irritating. In a word, love sums up these four qualities, but Paul adds a fifth which gives the reason for the others – 'eager to maintain the unity of the Spirit in the bond of peace' (3). Sadly, the desire to tell tales about our fellow Christians is more characteristic of us than the desire to build them up. It is the work of the Spirit to unite us: we *are* one in Christ as fellow-believers. However, it is an essential prerequisite of an effective church that this unity be actively maintained in the binding cords of peace.

So Paul turns to the seven basic affirmations of the Christian creed which bind us together. 'One body' – as long ago as 1884 H. C. G. Moule commented, 'Let the relations of practical Christian Life and Work correspond to that fact, to the utmost possible'. We are all possessed by 'one Spirit' and we share 'one hope'. There is 'one Lord' whom we all serve – Jesus Christ. This basic common allegiance to Jesus Christ is expressed in the earliest Christian creed (1 Cor. 12:3; compare 1 Cor. 8:6; Phil. 2:11). 'One faith' is shared by all; our basic beliefs and our basic allegiance to Christ are symbolically expressed and sealed in 'one baptism' which is the one Christ-given gateway into the Christian church. Finally, there is 'one God and Father of us all . . .'; 'above all' – he controls us; 'through all' – he cares and works for us; 'in all' – he is truly with us.

4:7-16 Diversity in unity

Having established the essential unity of the church, Paul now turns to think about its individual members. Just as Christ had given Paul grace for a particular task (3:2), so he has apportioned to everyone the necessary gift to fulfil his ministry. In order to underline his point, Paul quotes a passage from Psalm 68:18, using it in a very Jewish way. F. F. Bruce has pointed out that the psalm was associated with Pentecost in the synagogue readings. Certainly Paul sees its picture of the returning Lord triumphant after defeating the enemies of Israel as a picture of Christ's return to heaven (compare John 14:12-14). Having conquered his enemies, he returns in triumph bestowing gifts as he comes.

The Hebrew version of the psalm has 'received' for 'gave'. Whether Paul changed it himself as a legitimate extension of its thought, or whether, more likely, he was quoting a common Jewish understanding from the Targum, we can never finally decide. The application is, however, clear. The ascension of Christ resulted in the outpouring of the Spirit and his gifts. The list of his gifts differs from those in Romans 12 and 1 Corinthians 12 in being primarily concerned with church leaders – 'apostles, prophets, evangelists, pastors and teachers' (11). Michael Harper in *Let My People Grow* (Hodder, 1977, pp. 61ff) has recently argued that Paul isolates these 'gifts' because they are constitutive of all true Christian leadership, and are to be found in every healthy church. Whether such an interpretation is right or not, it is certainly true that all these people had had a key role in Ephesus in equipping the saints, the people of God, for their twin responsibilities of service and of building up the body. (The first comma in verse 12 is an unnecessary and misleading English addition, compare NEB.) So we have a picture of the gifts of leadership being given so that *all* may fulfil their ministry and so that the body may grow. The results of the proper exercise of such gifts are seen in verses 13-16. Everybody is united in their belief and in their personal knowledge of, and allegiance to, Christ. All are growing up *together* to be mature men in Christ – a maturity measured by nothing less than the standard of Christ himself. Childish whims and childish vulnerability (14), especially in matters of doctrine, are laid aside.

So, as Paul says in summing up his vision of the church, when each part of the body is doing its proper God-given job, is lovingly sharing the truth, then the body will grow in love, and grow to be more like Christ, its head.

Additional notes on Ephesians 4:11-16

1. The gifts of Christ to his church

The five gifts mentioned here are not immediately identifiable today. The term *apostle*, while having a wide meaning of 'a messenger' (one who is sent [Phil. 2:25]), is normally restricted either to the twelve or those who had been with Jesus in his earthly life and had seen the risen Lord (1 Cor. 15:7,8). If Paul uses it in this sense, as he does in Eph. 2:20, then there are none today. The apostolic commission is certainly given to the church, but that is another matter (compare M. Harper, referred to in the previous section). Closely associated with the apostles were *the prophets* – in *The Didache*, written about AD 70 or 80, the terms describe the same people. In the light of the Old Testament we must define a prophet as one who declares God's truth to a specific situation either under the immediate inspiration of the Spirit or through his 'Spirit-led' meditation on God's truth and its application in that situation. In that sense prophecy is still heard in the church, but just as the prophecy recorded in the Bible must be interpreted in its context, so we must guard against universalising a specific message and making it rival scripture in authority. *Evangelists, pastors* and *teachers* have an obvious meaning and an obvious interpretation. In spite of Michael Harper's stimulating comments, there is a good case, in view of the parallel thought in 2:20, for suggesting that Paul is speaking historically and is pointing out that both the earlier itinerant ministries and the later settled ministries, which have a more permanent function, are God's gifts for the building up of the church. If so, then we should see the modern parallel to the apostles and prophets as the initial carriers of God's message to a virgin mission field – the great 'church-planters' of the nineteenth and twentieth centuries.

2. The nature of Christian maturity

Three things stand out from this passage. First, maturity is achieved corporately. Paul's argument throughout these chapters is that we grow together and the Christian who tries to reach maturity on his own will be stunted. We need to guard against the individualism which seeks Christian maturity without thought of the growth of others. In no way can that be said to be a growth in love (16).

Secondly, the *pattern of maturity is Christ* and its aim is to share all the fullness of God in Christ (13,15). Ultimately the full glory of the risen and ascended Lord of which Ephesians speaks may only be experienced when our re-creation is complete, beyond the grave. Through his Holy Spirit, however, it is partially experienced now.

Thirdly, the use of 'mature manhood' (*eis andra teleion*, 13) and the similar 'one new man' (2:15) remind us that Christian maturity and human maturity are related qualities. Full and true humanity was found in Jesus – mature humanity is attainable only in Christ. The corollary also deserves thought – Christian maturity must include the realisation of our fully human potential. It is all too easy to talk of spiritual maturity as a quality which is unrelated to our essential humanity. Rather we need to recognise that the development of our human potentialities and the qualities that are recognised as 'adult' and 'mature' are basic to Christian maturity.

4:17-24 The old and the new

As Paul turns to consider the inner life of the church, he begins with a simple exhortation to live no longer like the Gentiles (17). He is, of course, writing to Gentile Christians but by his logic they are no longer Gentiles but members of the new Israel (compare 2:11-22).

Running through this exhortation is a concern with the mind and with thinking. Paul realises that the attitudes and conceptions of the mind are crucial for right behaviour. So the Gentiles are said to live 'in the futility of their *minds*' (17), 'they are darkened in their *understanding*, alienated from the life of God because of the *ignorance* that is in them' (18). In contrast his readers have *learnt* Christ (20). They were '*taught* in him, as the *truth* is in Jesus'; so they must 'be renewed in the spirit of (their) *minds*' (21,23). In stressing the place of thinking, Paul is not talking of intellectual prowess, but emphasising the vital fact that wisdom – an understanding of the truth as it is in Jesus and its implications – is vital for right living.

On the one hand ignorance leads to alienation from God and his life, the loss of sensitivity and compassion (18), callousness, licence and impurity. On the other hand, true knowledge of Christ, leads to 'the new nature, created after the likeness of God in true righteousness and holiness' (24).

The metaphor of changing clothes – 'put off', 'put on' – is a familiar one for Paul in this context. God's purpose is to create in Christ 'one new man' (2:15) – that is, the new humanity into which Gentile and Jew are brought. Here the old man of our sinful habits and attitudes is to be laid on one side and with renewed minds the new man is to be put on.

Greek has two words for new – *kainos*, usually meaning fresh, and *neos* meaning young. Both have verbal forms. Paul's command is to have *rejuvenated* (*neos*) thinking – 'be renewed in the spirit of your minds' (23) – and a *fresh* nature (*kainos*) – 'put on the new nature' (24) – which is like God in its righteousness and holiness (compare Rom. 13:14).

THOUGHT: Attitudes and conceptions of the mind are crucial for right behaviour.

4:25-32 Grieving the Holy Spirit

In the midst of a long list of down-to-earth instructions about the way we should treat each other comes this enigmatic command – 'Do not grieve the Holy Spirit of God' (30). It is accompanied by an echo of 1:13. In 1 Thessalonians 5:19 Paul has urged the Christians there not to 'quench the Spirit' – not to pour cold water on his fire. If the latter phrase refers to preventing the exercise of the Spirit's ministry through fellow-Christians, or oneself, the context of the former suggests that the things which grieve the Holy Spirit are the things which mar our relationship with our brothers in the Lord.

The whole of this passage is concerned with actions which affect another person. Don't tell lies because 'we are members one of another' (25) – it breaks our love and fellowship. 'Keep your anger for the right places and don't nurse it' seems to be the force of verse 26. If it leads to growth in the body all well and good, but if not then it is sin – it gives an opportunity to the devil. Stealing (28) obviously wrongs another; instead money should be earned honestly so that we can be generous to each other. Also stealing – taking another's goods – is the opposite of generosity – giving another yours! Speech (29) should profit those who hear it. Phillips and the RSV are probably nearest the mark in translating the phrase 'good for edifying . . .' as 'words suitable for the occasion'. In all these things, says Paul, by offending your brother you grieve God's Holy Spirit. You were, after all, *all* sealed with the Holy Spirit. He is your corporate guarantee (1:13,14) of your inheritance. His presence means you must live the life of heaven now; in the presence of God none of these things must happen.

Likewise all bitterness, wrath, anger . . . (31) must go. But Paul will not end on a negative note. The way not to grieve the Spirit is to honour him – by being kind, having real sympathy (empathy is perhaps the best word), and forgiving each other. But what a standard is set! It is 'as God in Christ forgave you' (32). The 'as' (*kathōs*) is a weak translation. Paul is echoing Jesus' searching words which stress the inseparable link between forgiving and being forgiven (Matt. 6:12,14,15; 18:21-35).

THOUGHT: The things which grieve the Holy Spirit are the things which mar our relationship with our brothers in the Lord.

5:1,2 Imitators of God

These verses really belong with the previous chapter (NB, 'therefore', 1) and sum up all that Paul has said about living together. Christians, in fulfilling their calling of being Christ to the world, are to become imitators of God. Greek scholars, trained in rhetoric, would recognise a familiar idea – the three essentials for learning the art of oratory were said to be theory, imitation and practice. Paul combines that idea of imitation with the concept of the relationship between a father and his children. In both cases the aim is not to produce the exact copy – no one could be that – but to form a character moulded by the same qualities and principles.

Nowhere in Ephesians do we have a hymn in praise of love like the one Paul had penned in 1 Corinthians 13. Love lies, however, at the heart of his argument. The love of God is the motivation of his action in Christ (1:5; 2:4; 3:18,19); a similar love must characterise his followers (1:15; 3:17; 4:15,16). So, in summary, Paul urges his readers to 'walk in love, as Christ loved us and gave himself up for us' (5:2). Again the 'as' translates *kathōs* (compare 4:32) – 'in the same way as' would better capture its force. To be urged to live a life characterised by love of the same quality as that of Christ is no casual thing. He was both 'the man for God' and 'the man for others' in unique fulfilment of the summary of the law which he quoted (Mark 12:29-31). This self-giving love was seen in all his life but especially in his voluntary death (2) – it is difficult to accept the suggestion of some commentators, that the reference is other than to his death. The word *paradidomi* has the basic meaning of delivering up to judgement or death and is frequently used of Jesus' suffering and death (see *The New International Dictionary of New Testament Theology*, Ed. Colin Brown, Vol. 2, pp. 367,8). So it is Christ's self-giving to the point of death which is our pattern and example. That was, in the Old Testament metaphor, a 'sweet savour' to God (compare, for example, Gen. 8:21; Exod. 29:18,25,41). The phrase is a poetic way of saying that it pleased him.

THOUGHT: Paul's exhortation is that love to the point of total self-giving must be the basic characteristic of all our mutual relationships. If that seems an impossibly high standard then it must be laid beside the equally staggering assurances of the earlier chapters (e.g. 1:23; 2:10; 3:14-20).

Questions for further study and discussion on Ephesians 4:1–5:2

1. How should we live as the redeemed people of God (4:1-3)? What is the difference between meekness and weakness?

2. What does 4:4-6 say about sects, denominations and church unity? See also 2:18-22.

3. How far do our church organisations and our own studies really encourage mutual growth of the kind Paul refers to in 4:11-16?

4. Have you any experience of the tossing to and fro referred to in verse 14? What was the cause? How was it counteracted?

5. If the mind is as crucial as Paul suggests in 4:17-24, what implications does that have for our church programme, and our own reading and study?

6. If one feels called upon to speak the truth, but cannot do it in love, what can one do (4:15,16)?

7. What is the cause of the Gentiles' alienation from God? What are the results? In view of verses 17-24 what should be our Christian approach to non-Christians? (Compare the comment, 'Human nature, contrary to much that is implied about it, is basically reasonable.') Carl Rogers insists that this is his certain conclusion, based on 25 years of work in psychotherapy. (*Why am I afraid to tell you who I am?*, John Powell, Fontana.)

8. 'Be angry but do not sin' (26). Give examples of when it is important to be angry. When is tolerance and the desire to avoid conflict a sin? When is anger a sin (31)?

9. What does verse 29 say about gossip? How would you define gossip? Discuss the comment, 'Prayer meetings are just gossip shops'.

5:3-14 Morals that matter

In the modern debate about sexual ethics the meaning of the words *porneia* (3, 'sexual immorality', NIV) and *pornos* (5, 'immoral', NIV) is frequently raised. What did Jesus mean in Matt. 5:32 by the exceptional divorce 'on the ground of *porneia*'? Do the words include homosexual acts and attitudes? – these are the questions asked by our age. William Barclay is certainly right in pointing out that the words must be understood against the Greek background of approval of prostitution, on the profits of which trade they built a new temple in Athens. 'We must remember,' he writes, 'out of what kind of society these Christian converts had come; we must remember with what kind of a society they were encompassed. There is nothing in all history like the moral miracle which Christianity worked.' This does not give us a precise definition of *porneia*, however. Perhaps it is meant to be a vague term and F. Foulkes may be right in suggesting 'it involves all that works against the life-long union of one man and one woman within the sanctity of the marriage bond'. The link with 'covetousness' (3,5) serves to remind us of the importance of the mind in sexual matters.

The blanket condemnation of verse 5 may seem strange after the stress on the possibility of reconciliation and forgiveness in Christ. Colossians 3:5-7 points out that the Colossians once went this way, so Paul is not denying the possibility of forgiveness. Nor is he suggesting that sexual sins are greater than others (the sins of the tongue are equally condemned in verse 4). He is rather expressing the radical change of character that Christ brings – it is unthinkable that a member of Christ's kingdom, one who has acknowledged his rule, could continue to live in this way.

Paul therefore likens life of this kind to darkness in contrast to the searching light of Christ (7-14). It is a common metaphor used by Jesus himself (John 3:19; 8:12), but Paul strengthens it – 'you were darkness, but now you are light (8). We are not just 'in the light'; we *are* light'! The acts of darkness are, to mix the metaphor, essentially 'unfruitful' (11) – that is, they do not profit or benefit anybody. Light, on the other hand, exposes what is there and allows it to be seen. The thought of this complex verse (13) seems to be that the Christian shows up the darkness around him and through his presence turns it into light – he brings forgiveness and renewal in Christ. So the light itself presents the challenge of the gospel – a thought which Paul sums up in a quotation (14) perhaps familiar to his readers (but not to us!). It combines his two metaphors of light and life, darkness and death.

5:15-20 Filled with the Spirit

Walking must have been a favourite pastime for Paul! Once again we are told to walk wisely and not as fools (compare 2:2; 5:2,8). The parallel passages in Colossians 4:5 and 3:15-17 make an illuminating comparison with these verses. In Colossians it is the Christian's behaviour towards outsiders which must be wise. Here concern about the life we lead has to do with time (16), thinking (17) and spiritual sobriety (18,19).

'Time' in verse 16 is *kairos* not *chronos*, opportunity not minutes (compare Gal. 6:10) and the NEB has caught the right nuance of – 'Use the present opportunity to the full, for these are evil days'. In the context Paul is perhaps urging his readers to use every opportunity to be a beacon for Christ in an evil world. If they are to do that, then, like him, they need a firm grasp of the will and purposes of God.

In 4:30 we were told not to grieve the Spirit; here is the positive command – 'go on being filled with the Spirit' (18). In total contrast to the pagan orgy of being 'full of new wine' we are to be totally under his divine control. This verse is often expounded as if the two halves were a comparison. Probably on the basis of Acts 2:13 it is suggested that one characteristic of being 'filled with the Spirit' is the kind of ebullience and self-abandonment which often goes with drunkenness. But the structure of the verse – drunkenness leads to *asotia* (wastefulness, uncontrollability and riotousness) while the continual filling of the Spirit leads to joyful songs and universal thanksgiving (19,20) – and the fact that 'self-control' is included among the fruits of the Spirit in Galatians 5 should warn us not to create points of comparison where Paul did not intend them. In context he is primarily concerned to draw out the contrast between the two states rather than any similarities!

Although the idea is not often associated with the verb, the present participle – 'go on being filled' – and the link between Spirit and wind (*pneuma* translates them both) suggest that the picture of a ship in sail is more helpful than that of a bottle! In order to move forward a sailing boat has to have its sails filled with wind. If we are to walk in love (5:2) and with due care (5:15) we must likewise be continuously filled with the Spirit. The picture of a bottle is far too static for Paul's understanding of the dynamic Spirit of God.

The parallel in Colossians 3:16,17 – 'let the word of Christ dwell in you richly' – suggests that in Paul's thinking there is a close association between allowing the gospel to make its home in our hearts and minds and being filled with the Spirit. Returning to the more common image, the person who walks in or by the Spirit is the person whose mind is shaped by the gospel of Christ.

5:21-33 Husbands and wives

'Be subject to one another out of reverence for Christ' (21) has both a backward and a forward look. Grammatically it looks forward; v.22 has no verb and must depend on the participle in v.21. On the other hand it follows the general principle which underlies much of what Paul has already said – if you reverence Christ, then you will respect your Christian neighbour in whom Christ lives – as well as underlying the specific marital situations to which he now turns.

In these days of 'Women's Lib.' the opening words of this passage may sound an alarm bell to some! But the heart of this passage, and its key, lies in v.32 – 'This is a great mystery, and I take it to mean Christ and the church' (compare 23,24,25,29). Paul sees the union of two people shown in Gen. 2:24 (31) as expressing in a human relationship the intimacy of Christ and his church. All his practical injunctions are worked out within that framework. So the 'subjection' of v.22 is only that expression of headship which is found between Christ and the church, between a head and its body. The essence of that headship and 'the basis of the passage is not control; it is love' (William Barclay). So vs.28,29 are a natural outworking of this principle. If we retrace our steps through the epistle and think of all that Paul has said about the relationship between Christ and his church, then the point is even more clearly established. There is no place here for a domineering husband; the emphasis is on the sacrificial love – Paul uses the Christian word *agapaō*, not *eraō* or *phileō* – which makes such a union possible (23,25,26). That was a revolution indeed to the Greek world where real companionship in marriage was scarcely known.

Within that context the role of the wife and the responsibilities of the husband are not a denial of women's rights nor a charter for male chauvinism. The mutual relations here described are to benefit the union. Husbands have a responsibility to 'nourish and cherish' their wives (29) just as Christ is the source of growth and love within the body (4:16). That is only possible if personal ambitions are subordinated to the corporate aims of the marriage: Christ's actions described in vs.25-27 as a pattern of the husband's love bear this implication. So the husband must place the care and support of the family high on his list of priorities – he cannot neglect that duty because of some personal whim. The wife must likewise put the family above *her* personal ambition. For most that will still mean subordinating career to care of the family, though in a changed social atmosphere the relationship of love and respect which Paul describes may find a different practical expression. The principles on which it is based, however, are timeless.

6:1-4 Children and parents

Continuing his discussion of family relationships, Paul turns to children. He once again uses an Old Testament text for support; on this occasion from the Ten Commandments (Exod. 20:12; Deut. 5:16). He interprets it specifically in terms of obedience (1) and uncompromisingly describes this as 'right'. F. Foulkes interestingly suggests the latter comment might be intended 'to carry the reminder that in some things children must accept and follow before they can see all the reasons'! The phrase 'in the Lord' is not meant to imply that sometimes obedience is not required if parental instructions are contrary to God's truth, but is simply a way of referring to the Christian family – Paul's theme in these verses.

The second half of the commandment is often forgotten but it is a reminder that the strength of family life and the upbringing of children are vital factors in the stability of a nation. In our own day this is possibly one of the most crucial challenges facing the church. The danger lies not only in the high incidence of marriages that break up, but also in the more insidious erosion of family life and loyalty through a variety of political and social changes which none of us can totally escape.

The complementary charge to fathers (4) is also a vital part of family responsibility. In Colossians Paul adds the extra phrase 'lest they become discouraged' (Col. 3:21). Whether he writes from bitter personal experience or not, he is obviously aware of the fact that disobedience and unruliness in children can easily be provoked by parental attitudes. The discouragement that comes from continuous rebuke and criticism is highly destructive of individual personality and growth. Instead Paul urges the right use of discipline and Christian correction – probably in the sense of training in the attitudes and standards of Christian behaviour. So the NEB, 'give them the instruction, and the correction, which belong to a Christian upbringing.'

THOUGHT: The strength of family life and the upbringing of children are vital factors in the stability of a nation.

6:5-9 Slaves and masters

Writing his apology around AD 150 Aristeides says: '. . . as for their servants or handmaids. . . they persuade them to become Christians for the love that they have towards them; and when they have become so, they call them without distinction brethren.' The principles of loyal and willing service and kind ownership here enunciated had truly taken root by the second century. Slaves were part of the New Testament household times, so naturally Paul includes instructions for them.

Once again his central concern is to place the outworking of the 'earthly' relationship in the context of the Christian's relationship with Christ whether he is slave or master. Obedience and respect (5) are to characterise the servants' attitude as if they were working for Christ (6-8). This will mean working 'wholeheartedly' (5), without drawing attention to oneself (6), and doing everything with kindness and good will (7). Masters, on the other hand, are to behave in ways that are worthy of that trust, loyalty and submission. The same basic principle (9) applies to them and God 'shows no partiality' – servants and masters are treated in the same way in his sight. How far these injunctions are applicable to modern industrial relations is a difficult question. Certainly the general principles apply, but the added factor of loyalty to one's fellow workers means that the outworking may well be different.

The question of the ethics of slavery and Paul's attitude to it have long troubled many Christians. Why was it left to Wilberforce to campaign for its abolition eighteen centuries after Paul? There is no slick answer, but certain things need to be said. First, it is quite clear from the words of Jesus and Paul (for example, 9) that they were aware of man's equality before God. Within the Christian community that equality was recognised and all were treated as brothers. Within the prevailing social order it was clearly different. Until the fourth or fifth century Christianity was a minority sect, hardly likely to influence the social structure of the Empire. Without our modern concept of democracy any attempt to abolish slavery would have been suicidal. The Romans were eager for excuses to persecute the Christians as subsequent history shows! Paul therefore concentrated on establishing Christian principles without always spelling out their full implications. Secondly, the factor which really roused Wilberforce's anger was *the trade* in slaves, the vast profits that were made in human flesh. The principle of having servants and employees did not. In this respect the eighteenth and nineteenth centuries were different from Roman times. Where the opportunity of freedom was given, as in Judaism, and treatment was fair, it was a more humane system than is sometimes realised. In a missionary situation, therefore, it was unlikely to be a priority.

6:10-17 The armour of God

Spiritual and inner strength was one of the central themes of Paul's prayer (3:16-21; compare 1:19). 'Be strong in the Lord' (10) echoes that prayer. Here as he draws his letter to a close, he reminds his readers why it is so important. The Christian life is a battle against a spiritual enemy. Our common opponent is not only described as cunning and subtle ('wiles', RSV, 11; compare 4:14) but also as 'the principalities and powers', 'the world rulers' and 'spiritual hosts of wickedness' (12). It is difficult to know precisely what Paul had in mind in using these terms but two things are clear. First, he sees opposition to the church in terms of personal agencies of evil, who possess great power and whose reign is worldwide. Secondly, he is concerned that we should not underestimate the enemy – we are not facing a merely human opponent (12).

The equipment, or armour, which God supplies is given so that we can stand firm. The verb to stand is repeated four times (11,13,14). The Christian must remain firm in his opposition. Each piece of armour refers to something Paul has discussed earlier in the letter. The equipment is God's own (compare Isa. 59:17) but entrusted to his followers. The girdle fastening the underclothing is truth. Paul has stressed its importance in ceasing to live as the Gentiles. The breastplate of righteousness comes from Isaiah 59:17 (compare 2 Cor. 6:7), but he has already urged his readers to 'put on the new nature, created after the likeness of God in true righteousness . . .' (4:24; compare 5:9). It is the necessary uprightness of character required of those who stand for Christ. 'The preparation of the gospel of peace' (15) is a strange phrase. NEB implies that the soldier must have a grasp of the gospel of peace to give him a 'firm footing'. The RSV seems to see it as part of the 'equipment' for battle. The former is perhaps better, especially in the light of the way the peace of the gospel has been expounded in chapter 2:11-22. 'For he (Christ) is our peace' (2:14) should govern its meaning here.

The implements of battle – shield, helmet (compare Isaiah 59:17) and sword are likened to faith, salvation and the word of God. Faith has always been central to Paul's argument as the means whereby God's blessings and promises are appropriated (1:13; 2:8). Just as the large Roman shield covered all the soldier's body, so faith in God's promises protects us and gives us assurance in the face of the doubts and aspirations of the evil one. Salvation is to be taken – it is the gift of God (2:8) – and affords great protection. The sword is 'of the Spirit' and in common with other New Testament writers Paul sees it in terms of God's own words (compare Heb. 4:12). We saw in 5:18 (compare Col. 3:16) the close connection in thought between the Spirit and the word of God. So here, the Spirit's and our weapon is God's spoken message – the truth we have to proclaim.

6:18-20 The importance of prayer

Comparison with Romans 8:15,16,26,27 shows that Paul thinks of praying 'in the Spirit' not as some special ecstatic prayer, but as the heart of prayer itself. (1 Cor. 14:15 contains a similar idea where Paul urges us to pray with both the mind and the spirit as one action.) So the overall protection against our spiritual enemy is prayer – inspired and prompted by the Holy Spirit himself. Just as the Christian life is life in the Spirit, so true Christian prayer is prayer in the Spirit. If we would truly pray we must do so under his divine influence, for in the Spirit we have access to God (2:18) and in the Spirit God comes and dwells in the church (2:22).

But prayer is never an easy occupation, and of that Paul is only too well aware. So he reminds his readers of the need to 'be alert with all perseverance', and to pray 'at all times'. Again the word is *kairos* with the idea of occasion or opportunity. Paul is not urging us to live life continually on our knees but saying that whenever the opportunity arises, we should pray. The man of God is the man who, in addition to his more regular times of prayer, has cultivated the art of using the odd moments of life to talk with his Lord and Master. Such prayer is not to be selfish. We are to pray 'for all the saints' – all our fellow Christians – 'and also', says Paul, 'for me' (19).

The substance of Paul's request is typical of the man. Yes, he is in chains, but he is still an 'ambassador', still God's representative. As he has expounded 'the mystery of the gospel' (compare 3:3,8-10) to the Ephesians, so now even in prison he wants to declare its truth boldly. He asks prayer both for the opportunity to speak – possibly mostly to his guards, though Acts 28:16,30,31 implies a greater freedom than we sometimes imagine – and for faithfulness in carrying out his God-given task (compare 3:2-5). If J. A. T. Robinson is right in his dating of the epistle (see introduction), then Paul's request is in anticipation of his defence before Felix and Festus and his decision to appeal to Caesar.

THOUGHT: Just as Christian life is life in the Spirit, so true Christian prayer is prayer in the Spirit.

6:21-24 Love undying

Paul writes to the Colossians (4:7-9) in almost identical words that his letter will be amplified by Tychicus (21). We know a little of this man. He came from Asia Minor (Acts 20:4) and 2 Timothy 4:12 confirms that he was sent to Ephesus, either with this letter or possibly another. He appears to have been considered as a possible relief for Titus in Crete (Tit. 3:12). All of these references confirm his loyalty and usefulness to Paul – 'the beloved brother and faithful minister (servant or deacon, *diakonos*) in the Lord' is obviously a deserved description. Here he is charged with the twofold purpose of passing on the news of Paul's welfare and of encouragement (22), an invaluable ministry amongst fellow-Christians.

Paul's letter closes with a blessing which echoes its opening note of peace and grace (1:2). The four virtues here – peace, love, faith and grace – have all been key themes of the epistle. There are two delightful phrases. First 'love with faith' (23). Probably the phrase is not meant to have any great theological significance but is simply a reminder that in true Christianity the two qualities are inseparable. Love springs from faith in Christ and love feeds faith and fidelity. We are probably all aware of the ugliness of faith without love and the possible fickleness of love without faith.

Secondly, his final words 'who love our Lord Jesus Christ with *love undying*'. The last word (*aphtharsia*) is used elsewhere of incorruptibility – incapable of decay (1 Cor. 15:42,50,53,54, compare Rom. 2:7; 2 Tim. 1:10). In other contexts it appears to be nearer sincerity or without corruption. Whichever translation we prefer, and the RSV seems to have the most support, the thought is reasonably clear – our love for Christ is to be both lasting and pure. Only such a love is an appropriate response to his love for us.

Questions for further study and discussion on Ephesians 5:3–6:24

1. Paul writes in ch.5 against a background of accepted immorality which his readers were in danger of absorbing uncritically. What contemporary sins which are accepted by today's society threaten us?

2. Bad habits and evil ways are not removed just by thinking about them and willing them to go, but by replacing them. What are the replacements Paul offers in 5:3-20? What others might there be?

3. 'The Christian shows up the darkness round him and through his presence turns it into light' (5:11). Have you any experience of how this works out in practice?

4. In 5:18 Paul says 'be filled with'. This is a command, but the verb is passive and present continuous. How do we let this happen – what suggestions does Paul make in 5:15-20 (compare Col. 3:16,17)?

5. 'Personal ambitions should be subordinated to the corporate aims of the marriage' (page 37). In your own experience what factors tend to disrupt family life? What do you find strengthens your family life?

6. Are there playgroup facilities and baby sitting services in your area? Do you know of any very lonely young mothers? Is there anything practical that your group can do to strengthen family life in your neighbourhood?

7. How far are Paul's instructions to slaves and masters applicable today? Do you agree that 'loyalty to one's fellow workers' makes a difference (page 39), and if so, how?

8. How are the 'wiles of the devil' experienced? What practical steps can we take to make full use of God's equipment, and to stand against the forces of evil in our day?

Introduction

Philippi was an important Roman colony in Macedonia. Paul travelled there in response to a vision (Acts 16:6-40). He crossed from Troas in Asia Minor to Neapolis, the port of Philippi, some eight miles south of the city and the end of the Egnatian Way, an important line of military communication with the East. This Roman influence is clearly seen in the terminology of the narrative in Acts and finds its echoes in the epistle (for example, 'citizenship', translated 'manner of life' in 1:27, and 'commonwealth' in 3:20, was an important Roman concept).

Paul and Silas were imprisoned because of the hostility their preaching aroused but Lydia, an immigrant seller of the prized purple cloth, and others, like their jailer, came to faith. Luke appears to have been left behind to carry on the work of building the church (the pronoun changes from 'we' in Acts 16:11, to 'they' in 16:40). Certainly by the time Paul wrote his letter the church had an established ministry (1:1) and a flourishing life. Paul obviously was especially fond of the church and this letter is perhaps the most direct and personal of all his writings. Most commentators suggest it was written from Rome, though Ephesus and Caesarea have their champions (see *The New Bible Dictionary*, pp. 98f, and J. A. T. Robinson, *Re-dating the New Testament*).

It has often been called 'the epistle of joy' because of the attitude Paul displays to his own suffering and his injunctions to the Philippians (for example, 1:4,19; 2:18; 4:4,10). His purposes in writing were probably many – to commend Timothy and Epaphroditus (2:19-30) and to thank them for their gift (4:10,14-18) are two of the more obvious. The main polemical passage in 3:2-21 concerns the threat from the Jewish 'circumcision' party – always a bone of contention in early Gentile Christianity. No introduction would be complete without reference to 2:5-11, one of Paul's clearest and most memorable statements of his understanding of the person of Christ.

Philippians: Contents

1:1,2 Greetings to the saints

Philippians shares with 1 and 2 Thessalonians and Philemon a unique place in Paul's letters. These four alone begin without any reference to his apostleship. There is just a simple personal introduction. As in other epistles Timothy is associated with Paul in his greeting, and their common description is 'slaves (*douloi*) of Jesus Christ' (1). The greeting 'Grace and peace' is usual in his letters but is no less significant for that – it combines the Greek welcome of *charis* – grace – with the Hebrew *shalōm* – peace – a positive quality of well-being and prosperity as well as the negative absence of trouble.

These opening verses are especially significant for the titles they use. 'Saints' is a common title for Christian people and reminds those at Philippi of their Christian difference. They are those who are 'holy (set apart) in Christ Jesus'. The expansion in the NEB, 'God's people, incorporate in Jesus Christ', bears little relation to the conciseness of the Greek phrase, *tois hagiois en Christō Iēsou*, but is theologically correct. Christians are set apart because they are God's people – chosen and commissioned by him. That process was achieved by incorporation in Jesus Christ of which baptism was the visible ceremony and sign (compare Col. 2:12).

The reference to bishops, *episkopoi*, and deacons, *diakonoi*, is unique in this context. The word *episkopos* means an overseer and is used synonymously in the New Testament with *presbuteros*, elder (Acts 20:17,28; Titus 1:5,7). But there is some evidence that 'elders' was a more general term for the senior men – its basic meaning is 'older men' – who ruled the congregation, while those who taught as well were known as 'bishops' (compare 1 Tim. 5:17; 3:2). However, such a distinction is tenuous and is probably more of a 'reading back' into the New Testament from the distinction which emerges in some churches in the second century. The bishops at Philippi and elsewhere shared a corporate responsibility for the spiritual well-being of the congregation.

Diakonoi, 'deacons', is a word that is used quite frequently for 'ministers' (for example, Eph. 6:21). Here they are quite clearly office-holders of some kind, though our knowledge of their precise function is not helped by the fact that the so-called 'deacons' of Acts 6 are only described in the verbal form as those who were to serve (*diakonein*) tables, while the apostles applied themselves to the ministry (*diakonia*) of the word (Acts 6:4): The qualifications, but not the function, of deacons are spelt out in 1 Tim. 3:8-13. Perhaps the vagueness of both terms can serve to remind us that there is no clear New Testament pattern of church government and therefore help us to adopt a more humble attitude to claims about any particular structure of ministry.

1:3-11 Joyful prayer

The affection that Paul has for the Christians at Philippi bursts out in these opening words. With a divine witness (8) he states that he longs for them all with the love and affection of Christ himself. It was quite literally a 'gut' reaction. The word for affection is *splanchna*. It described the internal human organs, in Jewish thought the seat of all the emotions. Such affection is based on a number of factors.

First, on his happy memories of his readers (3-5). Not just of his first meeting with Lydia, and the suicidal jailer, and their households, but also of their 'partnership in the gospel from the first day until now' (5). Whether this was simply in prayer or in the loan of Epaphroditus (2:25) is not clear, but so warm are his memories of them that every prayer on their behalf is always tinged with joy. Secondly, this partnership in Christ is a common sharing of grace (7) so that they share with him in his imprisonment and in his defence (his *apologia*) and confirmation (*bebaiōsis*, the establishment in a body of believers) of the gospel (7). The NEB has probably caught the nuance of Paul's thought that, although Paul is the one in prison, and the one especially entrusted with defending the gospel, they share in his unique privilege. All our tasks for God are shared in this sense; I may have a unique role but I never carry it out by myself, instead I do it in partnership with the whole church. Thirdly, his affection is based on the assurance that Christ will indeed fulfil his promise and the 'good work' he has begun in them will be brought to its fullness – its final destiny – at the day of Jesus Christ. This emphasis on the 'now, but not yet' aspect of Christian experience is characteristic of Paul and his doctrine of the Spirit. Through the Spirit we experience now the joys of salvation, yet that salvation is not complete. We have to work it out in practice (2:12) and wait to experience its fullness (6).

His prayer (9-11) is simple and to the point – that they may have ever increasing love, knowledge and discernment. This will enable them to be both pure and blameless for that secure future at the day of Christ, 'reaping the full harvest of righteousness' (NEB) which comes through Jesus Christ.

THOUGHT: Through the Spirit we experience now the joys of salvation, yet that salvation is not complete. We have to work it out in practice and we have to wait to experience its fullness.

1:12-14 The benefits of imprisonment

It is clear from passages later in the epistle that Paul sees himself at a crucial stage in his imprisonment (for example, 1:19-26; 2:17). This might fit better with the final phase of his detention in Rome than with his time in Caesarea or a conjectured time in Ephesus. It is hardly conclusive, however; to be in Roman hands under any circumstances was hardly likely to be pleasant and was bound to raise the question of survival. It is natural, therefore, that the Philippians should be concerned for Paul's welfare. His answer to their concern is to point out the benefits of his imprisonment. It has served to advance the gospel in two ways (12).

First, the gospel has benefited directly. Because he is where he is the reason for his imprisonment is known throughout 'the whole praetorium'. The word originally described the tent of the commander and hence came to be used of the army headquarters. It was also used of the residence of the provincial governor, and occasionally of the forces of the praetorian guards. If Paul was writing from Rome it could mean the Emperor's palace or his guards – he was after all in imperial custody. Whatever its precise meaning, Paul is aware that publicity in such places is strategic and therefore of great benefit to the cause of the gospel. One could paraphrase his comment by saying that the reasons for his imprisonment were well known both to the authorities and the general public – a notable achievement!

Secondly, the cause of the gospel has gained indirectly through the encouragement it has given to their 'brothers in the Lord' – it seems more natural to take the phrase 'in the Lord' as qualifying 'brothers' rather than 'confident'. Because of the way they have seen Paul react to his situation, his fellow-believers are boldly proclaiming the gospel – 'fearlessly and with extraordinary courage' (NEB). It has always puzzled non-Christians that persecution encourages and strengthens the church, but it remains one of the recurring facts of church history. In another context, Paul stresses that God works not in spite of weakness, but through weakness itself (2 Cor. 12:7-10; compare comment on Phil. 2:5-11 below).

1:15-18 Christ is set forth

The Christians in Rome are preaching with greater courage because of Paul's imprisonment. Paul is, however, aware that motives are mixed. So he points out that his joy is not thereby clouded; he rejoices that Christ is being proclaimed.

Some proclaimed Christ out of love (16). Because Paul was in prison they redoubled their own efforts to make up for his incapacity. Realising that he was there 'for the defence of the gospel' they made sure that the fact that it was, as it were, *sub judice* did not prevent its being heard and discussed. Others did so out of 'envy and rivalry'. Presumably they saw his imprisonment as an opportunity to further their own ends. Perhaps, as at Corinth, there were those in the area who wanted to stir up support for particular personalities or to advance their own position in the church. Paul's reaction is interesting. He welcomes the fact that Christ is proclaimed, perhaps because, unlike Corinth, he sees no danger in such activity dividing the church.

It is all too easy for us to do Christian work in order to draw attention to ourselves. We want our Youth Club, or whatever may be our responsibility, to flourish because we feel it reflects badly on us if it does not. That kind of thinking is totally absent from Paul's mind. Provided Christ is preached, then he does not mind who gets the credit or what reasons might lie behind the proclamation.

FOR SELF-EXAMINATION: Look at your Christian activities in the light of Paul's attitude.

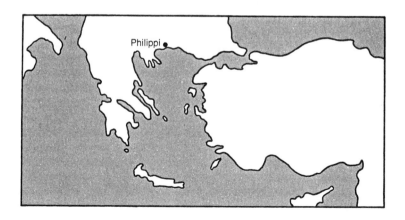

1:19-26 To live is Christ, to die is gain

It is not only the preaching of the gospel which causes Paul to rejoice, but also the assurance of his 'deliverance' (19) – the word literally means 'salvation'. There is a subtlety about these verses that can easily be missed. Many commentators see the thought of death which dominates verses 21-24 as detached from his confidence of 'salvation'. The point Paul is making, however, is that whether he lives or dies (20) he will continue to rejoice because Christ will be honoured. Yes, the Philippians' prayers were for his physical deliverance, but even if his salvation comes through death there is still cause for rejoicing. Paul does not relieve their anxiety with a false reassurance, like the 'we will soon have you home again' which we find ourselves saying to those with terminal illnesses. Rather he faces them with the full Christian hope that whatever happens, we can still rejoice, for our hope and expectation transcend the grave.

In fact, says Paul, Christ means so much to him in this life, that the thought of his more immediate presence beyond death is all gain (21). So, in a rare exposure of his inner turmoil and thinking, Paul reveals the debate of his own heart: to die and be with Christ or to live and continue his God-given task. On the one hand death would bring a personal advantage, on the other, life would allow him to complete his apostolic commission, especially with regard to them (23,24). It is the conviction that his work is not yet complete, that he still has a job to do to further their progress and their joy in the faith, that persuades him that he will see them again (25,26). This is not the false comfort referred to earlier, but a conviction based on a realistic appraisal of the situation (20-22) and an assurance of God's purpose. The fact that v.22b is in the first person singular should not lead us to imagine that Paul feels the choice is his. Rather we are allowed to enter into his personal debate – 'now which one would I choose, if the choice were mine?'

Whether Paul did see them again remains unknown. It depends partly on the date of the letter and the place of imprisonment. Titus 3:12 implies that even in his Roman captivity he had freedom of movement and hoped to be in Nicopolis in Epirus (on the western shore of modern Greece). But this is still a fair step from Philippi!

FOR MEDITATION AND PRAISE: . . . the full Christian hope that whatever happens we can still rejoice, for our hope and expectation transcend the grave.

1:27-30 Firm in suffering

In the meantime, Paul urges his friends at Philippi to do one thing – the 'only' has tremendous force ('this and this only') – to lead a life 'worthy of the gospel of Christ'. The word translated 'manner of life' (27) is the verbal form of the Greek word, citizenship (compare 3:20). Possibly it is a pun on their status as Roman citizens – a status of which both he and they were proud. The central thought is common to Paul's letters (compare Eph. 4:1; Col. 1:10). The practical details of our life must be moulded by the gospel of Christ. Only in this way can Paul be sure that, whether he sees them in the future or not, they will stand firm.

The characteristics of such a life are many, but Paul isolates two which he feels are important in the situation at Philippi, where there was clearly opposition to the gospel. First, there must be a united stand for the faith of the gospel (27). One of the more trivial memories I have of attempting to learn Latin at school is of failing to translate a short story entitled 'An old man teaches his son that unity is strength'. The story told how the old man asked his son to break a bundle of sticks. When he had failed he made him break each one on its own, which he did with ease. Unity is indeed strength, for Christians as well as sticks. Secondly, they must have courage to stand up to their opponents. The NEB and Good News Bible are probably right in their paraphrases of verse 28b. The implication is that the Philippian Christians' courage will, under God, prove to their opponents that they are doomed, while proving to the church that they themselves will be vindicated.

Their calling to suffer for their faith is to be regarded as a privilege – a matter of grace. The verb Paul uses is from the root *charis*, grace. Engaged in the same conflict as Paul himself, they share the God-given privilege of facing opposition and rebuke. In that context, too, a life moulded by the gospel is essential if they are to remain firm to its principles.

Questions for further study and discussion on Philippians 1:1-30

1. The whole of this chapter, as well as the letter, is characterised by joy. How many reasons for joy can you find in this chapter? What lessons can we learn to help us to be more joyful?

2. Persecution and imprisonment are inflicted on many Christians in some parts of the world. How does Paul's experience help us to understand? What are appropriate responses for us to make? How can we support and help Christians in these situations?

3. In what ways has an apparent tragedy in Paul's life been turned into a triumph? Have you any experiences that illustrate something similar (compare Rom. 8:28; 2 Cor. 12:7-10)?

4. 'It is all too easy to do Christian work in order to draw attention to ourselves' (page 49). How can we guard against this (1:15-17; 2:3-11)?

5. When people seem motivated by a desire to do us down (17), what can we do (1:18-21; 2:3-11)?

6. What is Paul's attitude to death? What is your experience of the attitude to death of non-Christians and Christians? What is the key to a lack of fear (23)?

7. Paul believes he will stay because he still has a job to do (24,25). Do you think it is true of every Christian that he stays on earth till he finishes the work God has for him to do? What is your work at the moment?

8. What will the Philippians' fearlessness demonstrate (28)? (Compare Acts 7:54-60). Why? Society today is characterised by fear. What are some of these fears? In what ways can your lack of fear challenge and help non-Christians?

2:1-4 Completing Paul's joy

J. Alec Motyer in *The Richness of Christ* gives these verses the titles 'Christian oneness' (1), 'Christian unison' (2) and 'Christian harmony' (3,4). Paul expands the point he has already made (1:27) that a life worthy of the gospel demands a united front. He begins by spelling out four reasons for such a unity – they are expressed in the words *paraklēsis* in Christ, *paramuthion* of love, *koinōnia* of the Spirit, *splanchna* and *oiktirmos*: encouragement, comfort, fellowship or common participation, affection and sympathy. The commentators differ widely in the way they understand the verse. Either it is to be viewed from the divine viewpoint – 'If Christ gives encouragement, if love gives comfort, if the Spirit . . .' (compare GNB) – or from the human viewpoint – 'If your life in Christ yields you any encouragement, if love has persuasive power, if fellowship in the Spirit means anything . . .'. Perhaps the best way of understanding the passage is to take 'in Christ' as a kind of title: If, in Christ, there is any encouragement, any comfort of love, any sharing in the Spirit, any compassion and sympathy (which there is!), then complete my joy, by expressing this through thinking the same things, through a common love, and through a common mind.

Such united thinking comes from having a right estimate of yourself – no selfishness – 'I *need* more' – or conceit – 'I *am* better'. Instead, always reckon that the other person is better and more deserving than yourself (3). The result is that you will always put the interests of others before your own. Here, in intensely down-to-earth terms, is the practical out-working of all the common privileges they share as those 'in Christ'. This is what love, affection and a common sharing of the Spirit are all about. If we took it seriously it could revolutionise our local church life.

THOUGHT: Always reckon that the other person is better and more deserving than yourself.

2:5-11 The Lord Christ

This justly famous passage begins with the phrase 'being in the form of God'. Most translations, like the RSV, take the participle as implying a contrast 'though he was . . ., he did not count' (6). Professor C. F. D. Moule, however, has recently pointed out that it could equally mean 'because he was in the form of God, he did not count . . .'. If this is so, Paul is stating that the humility which Christ exemplifies is of the very character of God himself. Christ, then, was in 'the form of God' – although 'form' can mean appearance, the Greeks understood it to mean not only the outer shell but the whole form within it. So he was what God was. But he emptied himself and took another 'form', that of a servant. The verb 'to empty' (kenoō) simply states that he 'freely exchanged his pre-existent, divine mode of being (6) for common, human, earthly existence' (*New International Dictionary of New Testament Theology*, Vol. 1, p. 547) compare 2 Cor. 8:9. As if that were not enough, 'being found in human form' (Paul uses another word for form, schēma [compare English 'scheme'] but with no significant difference in meaning) 'he humbled himself and became obedient unto death, even death on a cross' (8). Here in this action is expressed the full extent of his humility. Not only did he share the human condition to the extent of dying, but he died in possibly the most degrading way man has ever devised – nailed to a baulk of timber.

'Therefore God . . .' (9). There is no suggestion on Paul's part, especially if C. F. D. Moule's reading is correct, that God was not involved in the process of Incarnation. God's 'reaction' (J. A. Motyer), however, is to exalt him in two ways. First, by bestowing a name (compare Rev 2:17), in fact, '*the* name which is above every name'. To the Hebrew, names, especially the names of God, were an expression of character. Secondly, he is to become the object of universal worship and respect (10). The acknowledgement of his Lordship (11) is part of this universal homage. Obviously, in the present age of the church, many do not so respect him, but Paul looks beyond this world to the situation when Christ will be 'all in all' and when all things will be 'in subjection under his feet'. Some will voluntarily yield him their allegiance, others will have to acknowledge his authority, as the criminal is forced to acknowledge the authority of his judge. 'Jesus Christ is Lord' was the earliest Christian creed. In that phrase – possibly the 'name' of verse 9 – is summed up the essential Christian belief and allegiance.

The mind of Christ, then, is demonstrated in the humility and humiliation which, under God, becomes the path to glory. Jesus was not motivated by glory, however. He was expressing the essential character of God.

2:12,13 Working it out

Paul's hymn to Christ (6-11) could stand on its own, but in Philippians it is part of a larger argument. Paul starts by discussing the attitude we should have to each other if we are to stand firm in the gospel. Now with the 'therefore' of verse 12 he adds a corollary. Because of what Christ was and did, we must work out our own salvation with fear and trembling. (The opening phrase means, as the GNB suggests, 'as you obeyed me in my presence, so do so now in my absence.')

The connection may not seem immediately obvious, but the logic of his argument is this. We are called to be like Christ in all his humility and to match such an incomparable standard requires hard work. Here at the heart of Christian living is the paradox of grace once again. Our salvation is of God. Paul argues in Ephesians 2 that this is the gift of his grace. Yet if we are to attain the required Christlikeness we have to work at it. Moreover, such work is not undertaken casually, but 'with fear and trembling', for it is undertaken for God himself.

The resolution of this paradox is to be found in the following verse: 'for God is at work in you . . .'. Salvation is past, present and future. When Christ died our salvation was secured. However, although we *have* appropriated it by faith it has to *be* worked out in daily life so that one day it *will be* complete. But we are not left on our own, for God through his Holy Spirit is working in us 'to will and to do his good pleasure': he requires our earnest co-operation, for neither our personality nor our will is obliterated by God's Holy Spirit – we remain ourselves! The process of living as Christians involves the refining of our personality by the Holy Spirit and the attuning of our will to his. Only thus can we truly follow the example of Christ in all his humility.

FOR PRAISE, THANKSGIVING AND EXPECTATION: Your salvation, past, present and future.

2:14-18 Children of God

If you have ever tried to bring up children, you are only too familiar with the grumbling and questioning. 'Do everything,' says Paul, 'without wishing you hadn't got to (and saying so) and without asking "why?" all the time.' If you wish to be children of God that is the standard he sets; a standard that will mark you out amongst your fellow-men. The words used, 'blameless' and 'innocent', point to lives that are above reproach and criticism, that are what they profess to be, the lives of God's children. Only lives like this are worthy of Christ who was uniquely 'without blemish' (compare Eph. 5:27; Heb. 9:14; 1 Pet. 1:19).

The NEB and GNB follow the alternative translation for 'holding fast' (RSV). They take it to mean 'holding forth', and have 'proffer' (NEB), 'offer' (GNB), a thought which follows more naturally from the preceding phrase. Our task as lights in the world is to offer the gospel of Christ, by our behaviour as well as our words. The RSV, presumably, sees it as a further requirement for the children of God in a crooked and perverse generation (compare 1:27). In either case, Paul can be proud of them on the day of Christ for he will know that all his work on their behalf has not been in vain. There is probably no greater joy within the Christian ministry than seeing those you have been privileged to help along the Christian way standing firm for Christ in a trying and difficult situation. Compared with that joy, the fact of Paul's death or life (17) pales into insignificance. So, returning to a familiar theme, he urges his readers to rejoice in whatever happens to him (18). The phraseology of verse 17 is strange to our ears, even if the general meaning is clear. Paul borrows the language of sacrifice and describes his life as the libation – the cup of wine poured out in offering to a pagan god. The fidelity of the Philippian Christians is the sacrifice which they have already made by their practical loyalty to Paul (4:18) – Paul's own life is the libation poured over the altar.

2:19-24 Timothy – a man of worth

There is a startling contrast in these verses – a contrast which sets the man of real worth apart from the rest. It was Paul's damning judgement on others – for their sake mercifully unnamed – that 'they all look after their own interests, not those of Jesus Christ' (21). There could be no more telling rebuke, yet it is so easy to deserve it. When we are hungry and tired and relax in an armchair instead of visiting an elderly lady in hospital, or when we are in a hurry to get home before midnight and pass a stranded motorist on the A10, whose interests have come first?

Timothy, on the other hand, is genuinely anxious for the welfare of the Philippian Christians. Were the others only pretending to be concerned? For that reason Paul wishes to send him to the Philippians as soon as he knows which way his case is likely to go, so that he can relieve their anxiety on his behalf (23). Paul's other reason is to hear news of them (19) – news which he is sure will cheer him. Timothy has been like a son to Paul in his work for the gospel. Ever since Paul met him at Lystra (or Derbe) – Acts 16:1 is not clear – they had been very close together. At Philippi (Acts 16), Thessalonica (Acts 17:1-14), Corinth and Ephesus (Acts 18:5; 19:21,22) he was with Paul, and both Colossians 1:1 and Philippians 1:1 mention him as present during Paul's imprisonment. Small wonder, therefore, that he was associated with Paul in writing five letters (1 and 2 Thess., 2 Cor., Col. and Phil.) and was the recipient of two more. He was also Paul's regular 'errand boy' – going to Thessalonica (1 Thess. 3:6), Corinth (1 Cor. 4:17; 16:10,11) and to Philippi. He had amply demonstrated that the interests of Jesus Christ and his gospel came first.

THOUGHT: 'Timothy,' writes William Barclay, 'is the patron saint of all those who are quite content with the second place, so long as they can serve.'

2:25-30 The man who risked his life

Epaphroditus is one of those men who appear with tantalising brevity in the pages of the New Testament. He seems to have been a native of Philippi who was sent by the church to Paul with their gifts (4:18). Apparently in discharging this duty he became seriously ill – was the journey too much for him? – so that Paul could say that he risked his life in the work of Christ. Now that he is fit Paul returns him to his friends at Philippi. There is perhaps enough information here to give the imaginative an idea for a novel, but never a biography! It is not even clear whether he was intended to stay in Rome with Paul (v.25 – 'and minister to my need' – could be taken that way). If so, Paul writes to reassure the Philippians that his return is not cowardice or failure.

But even though we know no more, the terms in which Paul describes him are full of meaning. He is a brother, a fellow-worker and fellow-soldier; 'one who works and fights with me'. Such companions are very precious. Ideally we should be able to say that of all our brothers in Christ and they of us, but we do not regularly deserve it. He was the Philippians' messenger – the word used is that for an apostle (see Additional Note on Ephesians 4:11) – and minister to Paul's need. Again the word is interesting, instead of the more normal *diakonos*, Paul has *leitourgos* which the Greek world used for the benefactors of the state, those who had performed some especially significant service. The anxiety Epaphroditus had caused his 'home church' by falling ill (26) gave rise to a concern for them which it is delightful to see. So Paul sends him back to them with the glowing report that 'he nearly died for the work of Christ, risking his life to complete your service to me' (30).

3:1-7 A Hebrew of the Hebrews

Chapter 3 begins as if Paul were intending to end the letter. 'Finally, my brethren, rejoice in the Lord' (compare 4:8). The abrupt change of mood does not necessarily imply that we have two letters collated into one, as some have suggested. It seems more likely that Paul either received fresh news of the activity of the 'Judaising' faction in Philippi or that, because of some other more personal reason, he decided 'to repeat what I have written to you before' (1b, NEB). To do so, he says, is no problem for him and acts as a 'safeguard' (NEB) for them. It might even be that he had simply not finished the papyrus roll he was using and did not want to waste paper!

The Judaisers were Christian Jews who insisted that Gentile converts observe the Mosaic law and be circumcised. Paul describes them in scathing and sarcastic terms – they are 'the dogs', the description usually reserved by the Jews for Gentiles, 'evil-workers' and 'those who mutilate the flesh'. The important point to grasp is that the reality to which circumcision pointed is found in Christ (compare Col. 2:11-14). So spiritual worship (compare John 4:24), the praise of Christ and a lack of confidence in outward, fleshly acts are all marks of the true circumcision. The need for the outward sign has passed. In Colossians 2, Paul adds the further reason that baptism now signifies all (and more) than circumcision ever stood for.

As if to reinforce his point, Paul lists the advantages he himself has 'in the flesh'. The Jews could, after all, expect a Christian who knows nothing of Judaism and its practices to reject the outward signs. That criticism could never be levelled against Paul. He has, he argues, more reason than any one else for 'confidence in the flesh'. He was by birth an Israelite, and belonged to the élite tribe of Benjamin, Jacob's well-loved son (Gen. 35:17,18). His circumcision was conducted in accordance with the commandment to Abraham (Gen. 17:12; compare Lev. 12:3). 'A Hebrew born of Hebrews' implies he was among those in the Dispersion who had retained their Jewish language and traditions, when so many had become only Greek-speaking. If this were not enough, as a Pharisee he had strictly observed the law in all its detail (compare Acts 22:3; 23:6; 26:5). Here was the Jewish faith at its most demanding and Paul adhered to it completely. His zeal was typified by his persecution of the church – it was a burning desire to vindicate God. His righteousness was above reproach in Jewish eyes. 'But' (7) one meeting with the living Christ on a road to Damascus had changed everything. Instead of putting these qualifications to his credit, he had shed them all – had revoked every human claim to honour and merit – so that he might be accepted in and by Christ.

3:8-11 The gain of Christ

In these verses Paul expands the uncompromising assertion of v.7. Everything, not just his Jewish faith and upbringing, is 'loss' compared to the overwhelming advantage of knowing Christ. Such knowledge is not, of course, a merely intellectual acquaintance. Of the two Greek words for knowing, Paul uses the one (*gnōsis*, verb *ginōskō*) which speaks of *personal knowledge.* Here is the pearl of great price (Matt. 13:45,46), an intimate personal relationship with Jesus Christ. In a scientific world we are deceived into thinking that knowledge is an objective, impersonal acquisition. This is a deception, even in the scientific field where any 'proof' involves intuition, commitment and experiment. In terms of life itself it is grossly misleading. True knowledge of life and, supremely, of Christ stems from personal encounter and experience. To say that is to recognise that the subjective/objective division in knowledge is false – all true knowledge is personal and that involves both subjectivity (it is *my* knowledge) and objectivity (it is not limited by my horizons).

Looked at, then, from the point of view of such knowledge of Christ everything else is so much 'garbage' or 'refuse' (*skubala*, v.8). The aim of Jewish religion was to be righteous before God. Paul, in spite of his own assertion (6) had to reach the point where he realised that in fulfilling that aim all the things which he had prized so highly (4-6) were useless and that only in Christ could he be righteous. Such righteousness was not based on obedience to the law – a righteousness which would have been his 'own' (9) – instead it was a gift from God, appropriated by faith in Christ. This is justification by faith – the heart of the gospel – that a right relationship with God is given not achieved. So much for the loss, the gain (8) is 'to know him and the power of his resurrection . . .' (10,11). Such knowledge gives an awareness of the power of his resurrection in a renewed life; a *koinōnia*, a sharing of his suffering, both in the sense of participating in his death and its benefits and in the sense of being so united with Christ that our sufferings and ultimately our death become his. Finally, we will share his resurrection and the life he lives for evermore (11). In his whole life (and death) Paul is closer to Christ than he is to his closest earthly companions.

3:12-16 Pressing on to the end

There is a family of words in Greek based on the root *telos*. They are concerned with goals, ends and achievements, designating perfection and completion. In Jesus' final cry the word 'completed' or 'finished' (John 19:30) comes from this root. So Paul, thinking of his certain hope (GNB) of the resurrection of the dead, says that he has not yet received it nor has he reached his *telos* – is not 'perfect' (RSV). His God-appointed destiny and the full flowering of his personality remain for the future. His goal has yet to be achieved. This thought dominates his life so that he presses on to lay hold of it, as Christ has laid hold of him (12). There is a delightful play of language here as Paul applies to himself the injunction which he has already given to his readers (2:12,13). Paul pushes himself to attain his goal and make it his own, conscious all the time that Christ has made him his own.

He amplifies the point by likening himself to a runner in a race. First there must be no looking back: no race is won with a constant backward glance. So in the Christian life we must resist, as Paul did, the temptation to live in the past, for whether it is glorious or depressing, it removes our eyes from the ultimate goal. Instead we should be 'straining forward', reaching out for the things that lie ahead as the runner strains to reach the tape. He is flat out for the end. The 'centre of gravity' of these verses lies clearly in the future, as Paul changes the metaphor slightly to contemplate the prize (compare 1 Cor. 9:24) which awaits those who continue to respond to the upward call of God. In an age which hankers after instant holiness and immediate achievements these words of Paul provide a necessary caution. We have never arrived as Christians – the goal is ever before us, the call is ever 'upward'. Neither is the way there easy – all the verbs Paul uses describe effort and energy, the total engagement of all our faculties in the pursuit and achievement of our *telos*, our ultimate goal.

Paul could rarely resist a play on words; verse 15 is no exception. Literally translated this says, 'As many therefore as are perfect (*teleios*), let us think in this way'. Yet Paul has just argued that perfection lies in the future! However, his meaning is clear. Let those of us who are mature, who are on the road to perfection, share this thinking. If we do not, God will expose our failure. Paul's final comment (16) shows that the one thing we must not do is to slip back. We must never prove false to that partial image of the *telos* which is already ours.

Questions for further study and discussion on Philippians 2:1–3:16

1. Paul repeatedly urges the Philippians 'to be of one mind' (2:1-11). What causes differences of opinion? When are they wrong? What is the right place for individual thinking and how is a common mind to be reached?

2. Give some specific instances of Christ's humility. If he were on earth now what would be the modern parallels?

3. No selfishness and no conceit (2:3,4, compare 2:2). 'This is what love, affection and a common sharing of the Spirit are all about. If we took it seriously it could revolutionise our local church life' (page 53). Can you suggest how your church life would be changed if everyone took this seriously?

4. What do the words 'Jesus Christ is Lord' mean? How can you demonstrate their truth in your life?

5. 'God is at work in you to will his good pleasure' (2:13,14). Sometimes it feels as though our churches are full of people doing jobs reluctantly because there is no one else to do them. How can we know when we should take on a position in the church, and when we should refuse?

6. What qualities characterised Timothy and Epaphroditus? How would you respond to someone who said, 'John is no good, he is an also-ran'?

7. Try re-writing 3:4-6 as if you were a modern Paul.

8. What 'gains' might we have which could prevent us coming to Christ? How far do our attitudes to money, ambition and time reflect 'the surpassing worth of knowing Christ'?

9. If someone said to you, 'How can I know Christ?' what would you say?

3:17-21 A tale of two cities

The slightly cumbersome language of verse 17 is better expressed by the NEB. 'Agree together . . . to follow my example. You have us for a model; watch those whose way of life conforms to it.' The reason is that we belong to 'a commonwealth' (20). We must live as citizens of heaven. Paul's use of his own example could be easily misunderstood. He has already hinted at it (15) but here it is openly stated. The thought is so daring that at least one commentator suggests it should be translated, 'Become fellow-imitators with me in imitating Jesus Christ'. While most of us would rightly prefer to make that statement, however, Paul almost certainly meant what the English translations say! He is constrained by the thought of those, presumably professing Christians (otherwise the contrast would lose its point), who are living to all intents and purposes as enemies of the cross of Christ. Their attractive example is not to be followed. Today we rightly recognise that our ministers and clergy are human. Perhaps in doing so we have lost a necessary emphasis, for it is their responsibility to be exemplars of authentic Christian faith and life. It was the need for a continuing embodiment of the faith and life of Christ which shaped the Christian ministry in the second century. While the memory of Christ and the apostles remained fresh such a structure was not so necessary; as the memory receded so the need increased. This is the real meaning of Apostolic Succession.

In contrast to Paul, the aims and goals of these other professing believers are totally human and earthly. Their thinking is fixed on this world, their god is their belly and their *telos,* their destiny, is destruction (19). The resurrection life which formed Paul's *telos* is not known among them. They remain citizens of the world while Paul and his imitators are citizens of heaven. To make his point, Paul deliberately chose a word pregnant with meaning for the Philippians. Although they lived in Macedonia and many were Macedonian by birth, they were Roman citizens by virtue of being a Roman colony. They were almost too literally an outpost of Rome in a foreign land, living in a Roman way, executing Roman justice and speaking the Roman language. So with us – we are heavenly citizens – an outpost of heaven on earth; we look forward to welcoming our deliverer who will grant us the full benefits of that citizenship (21) – a theme Paul was to develop in Ephesians. As there (see Eph. 1:19-23; 3:20) the power which makes it possible is demonstrated in Christ's universal reign.

4:1-3 The true pastor

The final chapter of Philippians contains a number of short, pithy comments about the situation in the church. Unfortunately, most of them are far too sketchy to give us any clear idea of the details of the matters to which Paul refers. Nevertheless they reveal both Paul's intimate knowledge of the situation – helped presumably by Epaphroditus (2:25) – and his concern. Here are the heart and words of a true pastor.

The chapter begins with a further exhortation to stand firm (compare 1:27; 2:16). Paul's description of the Philippians as his joy and crown contains the thought of the victorious athlete or the privileged guest at a feast (the Greek word for crown, *stephanos*, is used for a victory wreath and a festive garland). So Paul pictures his readers as his reward for winning the race; his festal crown at God's great banquet. Unity was a central thought on the first occasion in which he urged them to stand firm (1:27). So here he turns to address one divisive situation. Of Euodia, Syntyche, Clement and the person who is called a 'true yokefellow' we know nothing, unless the last is a reference to Epaphroditus. The description of their work with Paul (3) might suggest that, like Lydia, they occupied an important place in the life of the growing church at Philippi. The phrase 'true yokefellow' could also be a name *Sunzogus* with the 'true' implying that his name is apt. Or could it be that Paul is laying on Epaphroditus as the bearer of the letter the responsibility for sorting out the dispute? Whatever its true meaning or the source of the disagreement, it is clear that Paul regarded such matters as of wide concern. With loving care Paul urges them to take to heart all that he has said earlier in his letter (2:1-4). Division harms not just the people involved, but the whole church. It is therefore appropriate that the church should be involved in sorting it out. Their agreement, moreover, is to be 'in the Lord', a reminder of the unity which Christ alone can bring. Few human organisations could attempt, let alone succeed, to bring together people from all walks of life, all cultures, races and languages. Yet that is the aim and achievement of the Christian church. That such exhortations as this exist (4:2) is not an admission of failure but a necessary reminder that we are human: our unity remains 'in the Lord'.

4:4-7 The peace of God

Having dealt with a specific situation, Paul now turns to a series of exhortations and a promise. The exhortations are not obviously connected, except by the fact that all three – joy, gentleness, lack of anxiety – are qualities which Paul feels are especially appropriate in the Philippian situation.

Joy on Paul's part has been a constant theme of the letter (for example 1:4,18; 2:17; 4:1). So as he concludes he returns to this thought. The Christian is one who has learnt, whatever the circumstances, to rejoice in Christ (compare 4:10-12). Such joy is not the passing effervescence of much human celebration but the deep underlying confidence in God and Christ that led Paul to sing praises in the Philippian prison (Acts 16:25). It sees beyond the immediate circumstances to the reassuring purpose of God. Just as a happy marriage is based not on the inevitable tiffs and frictions on the surface, but on the deep underlying love, trust and security between husband and wife, so the Christian, who is called to face the vagaries of life, can do so with joy because of the underlying love, trust and security between him and Christ.

Every so often one comes across a word which has no precise equivalent in English; *epieikēs* is such a word. Forbearance (RSV) is perhaps the least misleading translation, magnanimity (NEB), with its implied condescension, perhaps the most. It is the quality that Jesus displayed in his dealings with the woman taken in the act of adultery – a quality of justice tempered by mercy. It is the gracious gentleness of the person who does not always demand his pound of flesh. It is the word used by Tertullus in addressing Felix (Acts 24:4; 'kindness', RSV); and to describe the kind and gentle masters in 1 Peter 2:18. It is one of the essential qualities for bishops in 1 Timothy 3:3. Such gentleness and consideration, says Paul, is to characterise all our relationships, because 'the Lord is at hand'. Although the Greek has no link, this is probably the sense of Paul's comment. The return of Christ reminds us of the shortness of life and the coming judgement of God. 'Vengeance is mine, says the Lord, I will repay.'

Paul's third exhortation is negative, 'do not be anxious', but unlike the unsuccessful, 'don't worry', we often use, he adds the positive steps which lead us to that freedom: prayer, for ourselves and for others, tempered with thanksgiving. It is so easy to underestimate the strengthening effect of thankful prayer that we continually need such apostolic encouragement.

These three qualities demonstrate the presence of the peace of God which keeps guard over our emotions and our thoughts (7, compare 2 Cor. 11:32 which uses the same military word for 'keeps guard').

4:8,9 The Christian mind

Paul frequently stresses the importance of the mind (see Eph. 4:17-24; Rom. 12:2). So here his final comments to his friends concern the things that should occupy their thinking. Because we are in mission to a non-Christian world we should be aware of secular thought. It has long been a principle of missionary activity that we need to study the culture and the situation to which our message is addressed. But if we wish to feed our minds and help them to become like the mind of Christ, then we must 'ponder' those things which are consistent with Christian thinking. In v.8 Paul lists the adjectives which describe these things – true, honourable, just, pure, lovely, gracious; such things are excellent and worthy of praise. Before applying these adjectives to the sphere of art, Professor Rookmaaker described them as 'the norms for man' and as 'expressing the true humanity which Christ came to restore' (H. R. Rookmaaker, *Modern Art and the Death of a Culture*, IVP, 1970, pp. 236ff). What then are these norms?

First, things which are *true*. We are surrounded by unreliable reports and biased comments, and live in a world where much is deceptive and illusory. We should set our minds on things which are reliable. Secondly, *honourable* (*noble*, NEB). The word is *semnos* which is normally used of the Greek gods. It describes that which is worthy of reverence, 'which has the dignity of holiness upon it' (William Barclay). *Just* describes things which are right, which ought to be done. *Pure* describes the moral purity or ceremonial purity of things that are fit to be used in the worship of God. In a world full of sordid thoughts and behaviour such purity is a rare and desirable quality. *Lovely* is best translated as 'winsome' (William Barclay). Sadly, that word is rarely heard today. The adjective describes the attractiveness of character and charm of the person 'whom to see is to love' (William Barclay). Finally, *gracious* is often linked with speech, hence the KJV 'of good report'. It perhaps describes all that is fitting to the occasion.

Their thoughts, then, are to be occupied with these things, while their actions are to be modelled on the teaching and example of Paul himself (compare 3:17). In both their thoughts and their actions the God of peace will be with them (compare 7). This is Paul's favourite title for God (compare Rom. 16:20; 1 Cor. 14:33; 1 Thess. 5:23); it stresses the security and prosperity that God alone can bring. Perhaps Paul uses it because he is conscious of the ever-present threat of division and disharmony.

4:10-13 Christian contentment

One of Paul's reasons for writing to the Philippians is to say 'thank you' to them for their kindness to him. They had ministered to his need by sending Epaphroditus (2:25), and in this way had shared in his trouble (14). Their generosity, however it was expressed, gives him another cause for rejoicing. Knowing that he has been in their thoughts he now rejoices that they have found a way to express their concern. Perhaps as he writes Paul is aware that they could infer from his remarks that he had been in need – a need which they had failed to meet. He therefore adds the justly famous words of v.11.

Paul's great lesson has been in the art of contentment (*autarkēs*). This quality of self-sufficiency was highly valued by the Stoics – a school of Greek philosophy which extolled the value of 'the stiff upper lip'! The pinnacle of their aspirations was to be totally independent of other things and people, a point they sought to reach by removing all desire and emotion. This was achieved through a rigid belief in the determinism of the gods. Paul's contentment is radically different. He has learnt to face everything and do anything with the strength that Christ alone can bring (13). It is not the abandonment of desire and emotion but its fortification and direction which brings his contentment. It is not self-sufficiency but *Christ-sufficiency* (compare 2 Cor. 12:10).

In an age dominated by materialism and wage-bargaining such an attribute is hard to cultivate. It is the ability to be content with enough; it is an attitude which threatens the very basis of our acquisitive society. Paul would be the last to deny that we need to provide adequately for our dependants, that employees should be paid a fair wage and that poverty should be alleviated. But the crucial words are 'fair' and 'adequate'. Not only do our ambitions make us desire more than we need, but also our standards of adequacy are all too easily affected by the fads and fashions of the world. One of my childhood heroes was Romany (G. K. Evens was his real name, I think), who as well as being a great naturalist was a Methodist preacher. He remarked on one occasion, when reproved for wearing old clothes – 'What's wrong with a patch?' What indeed? He knew the secret of contentment, which he defined as 'holding together one's mind, body and soul in equipoise'.

4:14-23 Generous giving

The Philippian generosity was well known, so much so that it irritated the Corinthians (2 Cor. 11:7-12). It is clear that from the moment Paul left them and travelled to Thessalonica, Beroea and Corinth (16; 2 Cor. 11:9) they and the other churches of Macedonia regularly contributed to his needs. It was Paul's boast that he had never been a burden to the churches he visited, but made enough by tent-making to support himself. Undoubtedly the extra gifts from the Philippians must have been a great help. Here he repeats his constant cry that he did not seek such gifts (17), his only concern was that they should learn the benefits of generosity (17, compare Acts 20:35). So great was their generosity that he could say he had received 'full payment' – the word regularly used to cancel a bill. Not that they owed *him* anything – rather their gifts were an offering acceptable to God (18). Their reward lay in knowing that and in the assurance that God is no man's debtor (19). Almost echoing the language of Ephesians, he assures his friends of God's generous care and offers his final ascription of praise to the God who is the Father (20).

In conveying his greeting to the church, Paul unusually used the singular 'saint', though in a corporate context – every saint. Elsewhere, he always uses it in the plural (compare v.22). Perhaps he writes in this way to emphasise that he wishes his greetings to be given to each member of the church individually. To his own greeting he adds those of his immediate companions and of all the saints, including those in Caesar's household – perhaps the strongest hint that it was written in Rome, though this is not conclusive.

The substance of his greetings echoes the opening words of the letter, 'Grace to you and peace from God our Father and the Lord Jesus Christ' (1:2). Here the direct link with Jesus Christ expresses his central belief in the gospel as the free gift of Jesus Christ. We all need that grace if we are truly and faithfully to live the Christian life. So Paul takes leave of his friends with the confident assertion that the grace of Jesus Christ will be at the centre of their lives. Sometimes in praying the fuller grace of 2 Cor. 13:14 we tentatively say 'May the grace . . . be with us'. But the Greek does not supply a verb. Perhaps it is both grammatically and theologically correct to see these verses as a statement of Christian fact – 'The grace of our Lord Jesus Christ is with you'.

Questions for further study and discussion on Philippians 3:17–4:23

1. What does it mean for you in practical terms 'to press on toward the goal for the prize of the upward call of God in Christ Jesus'?

2. The Philippians were in the middle of persecution, so why should they rejoice? What reasons do we have for rejoicing?

3. Young children want to prove themselves to others, but Christians should be free from the need to justify and be understood. Why (4:5)? Give examples of the working out of gracious forbearance.

4. Oswald Chambers has said that worry is a form of 'unconscious blasphemy' – why is this so? What is the antidote to worry (6)? Can you share some experiences of ways that God has provided for your needs (19)?

5. What implications does 4:8 have for our work and leisure?

6. How has Paul learned contentment (11-13)? In what ways do you have to learn contentment in your own life?

7. Much of modern society is based on greed, which takes many forms. In what ways does being 'content with enough' threaten the basis of our contemporary materialistic society (page 67)?

8. Some Christians are characterised by an outgoing generosity. Illustrate from this letter the forms that this can take. Why do you think it irritated the Corinthians (page 68, 2 Cor. 11:7-12)?

9. This is a very personal letter in which Paul reveals much of himself. What would you say are his outstanding characteristics which we should imitate (3:17)?

Introduction

Colossae was a town in the province of Asia, on the road east from Ephesus. It lay in the Lycus valley near Laodicea (see 4:16) and its inhabitants probably heard the gospel while Paul was in Ephesus (compare Acts 19:10). Unlike most of Paul's other letters Colossians was written to a church which he probably never visited (compare 2:1). This is reflected in the opening chapter where he speaks of their hearing the gospel from Epaphras (1:7) and of his hearing of their faith and love (1:4,8). His reason for writing, however, appears to be the report that they may be open to the danger of accepting a mixture of Christianity with Jewish ideas and pagan philosophies (see notes on 2:8-23). Such syncretistic doctrines were later to emerge in the fully-fledged systems of Gnosticism. These second-century heresies attempted to solve the problem of evil by drawing on Greek philosophy and Persian cosmogony to create a series of different explanations of the origin of the world and of evil. These heretical beliefs shared a dualistic concept of reality in which two gods existed – one good, one bad – and in which matter was inherently evil. Thus they denied the possibility of the Incarnation. Whether the Colossian heresy was an early form of one of these heresies is not clear. All one can say is that certain elements of Paul's teaching and warnings fit a background of 'a kind of "theosophy" – in this instance, a "gnostic" type of Judaism or a Jewish type of "gnosticism"' (C. F. D. Moule, *Colossians and Philemon*, CUP, 1958).

To counter this threat Paul's teaching contains some of the most striking words in the New Testament about the person of Christ and his position in relation to the universe and the church. The letter is also notable for its contribution to our understanding of the nature of the church itself and of the process of becoming, as well as the meaning of being, a Christian. These are the great themes of the letter. We have already noted the parallels with Ephesians. Perhaps the threat of heresy at Colossae meant that Paul wrote with greater urgency and more daring metaphor. It was probably written from Rome, about the same time as Philemon and Ephesians, though again Caesarea and Ephesus have their champions.

Colossians: Contents

1:1,2 Greetings to the saints

The structure and content of Paul's greeting is familiar from Ephesians 1. There are two minor variations. First 'Timothy, *the* brother' is included with Paul in sending the greeting (compare note on Phil. 2:19-24). Such an association is common in Paul's letters but is perhaps surprising in this context as we have no evidence that Timothy ever visited Colossae, although he would be well known in Ephesus.

Secondly, Paul addresses 'the saints and faithful brethren in Christ at Colossae'. Professor Moule feels that *hagiois*, 'saints', is best taken as part of the description of brothers as the article is not repeated before 'faithful'. If this is correct the phrase then reads, 'To the dedicated and faithful brethren in Christ at Colossae', or, as Professor Moule renders it, 'a brotherhood dedicated and loyal to God'. Such a translation strengthens the idea of the church as God's own people. The additional phrase 'in Christ' is a reminder that their brotherhood is through 'incorporation' in him. Once again, then, Paul establishes his divinely ordained credentials and in his description of his readers identifies himself with them as part of the people of God.

1:3-8 Epaphras – a reason for thanksgiving

Paul's prayer for his Colossian readers begins in v. 9 preceded by his reasons for giving thanks. Such an expression of thanksgiving is a regular feature of Paul's writings, occurring in all his letters except Galatians, 1 Timothy and Titus. The reasons are clearly stated. He, or they, if the 'we' (3) is meant to include Timothy, has heard of their faith as those incorporate in Christ and of their love for all God's people (one of John's marks of authentic Christianity [1 John 3:14]). The next phrase, 'because of the hope . . .' could either refer to the basis of Paul's thanksgiving or of the Colossians' faith and love. Grammatically the second is more likely. Christian hope is no vague wishful thinking, but the secure confidence that is ours 'in Christ'. It is therefore the opposite of escapism – it is the foundation of our trust and love in the present. So Paul's thanksgiving is centred on the three great Christian themes of faith, hope and love (1 Cor. 13, compare 1 Thess. 1:3).

It was Epaphras (7) who had told Paul of their love, which is described (8) as *en pneumati*, either 'spiritual' in the sense of more than human, or 'in the Spirit' (RSV), meaning in the sphere of the Spirit or inspired by the Spirit. 'Epaphras' could be an abbreviated form of Epaphroditus (compare Phil. 2:25), but there is no reason to identify them. The former is mentioned twice in Colossians (1:7; 4:12) and once in Philemon (23). He appears to have come from Colossae and to have brought the gospel to his own people (7). Paul argues that they had heard of their hope 'before' (5) through the gospel. If 'before' applies to the heresy, i.e. they had heard the gospel first, then verse 5b should probably read, 'Of this you heard before in the real (true) gospel which has come to you.' This good news, like the Colossians themselves (10), is bearing fruit and growing. In terms reminiscent of the parable of the sower Paul reminds them of the remarkable spread of the 'true understanding of the grace of God' (6) both in Colossae and elsewhere.

THOUGHT: Christian hope is no vague wishful thinking but the secure confidence that is ours 'in Christ'.

1:9-14 Prayer for discernment and strength

C. F. D. Moule has helpfully pointed out the structure of Paul's prayer. First, 'the actual *petition* is for: (9) a sensitiveness to God's will consisting in a grasp of what is spiritually valuable, (10) issuing in conduct worthy of Christians, and pleasing to Christ . . .; (11) the equipment for this being strength, a strength derived from God's power . . . a strength which cheerfully stays the course. Then comes *thanksgiving* – (12-14) for light, for love, for rescue from evil. But the prayer has already sprung out of an *antecedent* thanksgiving: its foundation is the solid fact of what God has done (alluded to already in verses 5-7), and to this it returns in verses 12-14'. He points out that in the numerous prayers of the New Testament the basis for prayer is always the solid fact of God's activity.

Paul's prayer is, moreover, intimately related to the Colossian situation. The request for discernment is necessary in the light of the philosophies which beguile them; in that context, strength is essential to carry out God's will. Paul's first request concerns their knowledge of God's will. This is not an intellectual grasp of the facts about God and his intentions, although it certainly involves the mind, but is rather the intimate personal knowledge which stems from an entrance into God's mystery – 'Christ in us' (1:27). Such knowledge is always intensely practical and cannot but result in a transformed life which is fruitful and pleasing to God. It is not clear grammatically whether 'in the knowledge of God' should be taken with 'increasing' as RSV (10) or whether it qualifies the whole verse – 'bearing fruit and increasing in every good work by means of the knowledge of God'. Paul's prayers are never simple to unravel, though the essential meaning is clear! Strength is his second request (11). 'The great problem of life', writes William Barclay, 'is not to know what to do but to do it'. The source of strength is the glorious might of God, and the result is seen in confident endurance and joyful long-suffering. So Paul completes his prayer (12-14) with a recital of what God in Christ has done for us. To be a Christian 'qualifies us for an inheritance', for we are part of the family of God; it gives us redemption, in the sense of present forgiveness (14), because we have been transferred into the kingdom of God's Son.

1:15-20 Christ over all

The section may be short but it contains within it some of the most profound teaching about Christ in the whole of the New Testament. Recent writing on Christology has likened the ascription of divinity to Christ to that of Buddha (see *The Myth of God Incarnate*, ed. J. Hick pp. 168ff). But the Buddha never claimed to be divine and the development of Mahayana doctrine took place 500–600 years after his death. Here we have a statement identifying the executed man of Nazareth with 'the image of the invisible God . . .' written less than thirty years after his death. That by itself, of course, is not an ascription of divinity – man is after all made in God's image, but there are clear divine implications both here and elsewhere in Colossians. At the end of verse 16 Paul adds to his usual thought of Christ as *the agent* of creation ('through him') the extra comment that 'all things were created . . . for him' (*eis auton*). This phrase had been used in Romans 11:36 and 1 Corinthians 8:6, but of God and not Christ. The statement here that Christ is the goal or purpose of creation is unique. A similar thought is present in 3:11 – 'Christ is all and in all' – in 1 Cor. 15:28 it is the description of God himself.

Christ's relationship to the created order is first spoken of in terms of his being first 'the first-born of all creation' (15). This was one of the verses which led the Arians of the fourth century to include Christ within the created order. But to interpret it that way is to flout the context (compare vs.16,17). It should therefore either be understood as meaning 'born before' creation or, more likely, as applying to status not time, an aspect of the title which is important in the Bible (for example Jacob and Esau, Exod. 4:22; Deut. 21:15-17; Ps. 89:27; Jer. 31:9). Christ, then, is *supreme* over all creation. Secondly, he is both the agent of creation and, with God, the one for whom it was created (16). Thirdly, the coherence of the world depends on him. Without his agency and activity the world would not hold together (17). Fourthly, he is said to be 'before all things'. This could be a priority of importance, but if so would be repeating v.15. That does not make it impossible – we all repeat ourselves! – but it adds weight to the other possibility, which is more common in the New Testament, that the Greek word *pro* indicates a priority of time. The phrase therefore suggests his pre-existence.

1:15-20 Christ and his church

Christ's relationship to God is spoken of first in terms of his being 'the image of the invisible God'. Man was, of course, made in the image of God, as we have already noted, but the inclusion of the word 'invisible' perhaps gives an added point. God is 'seen' in the created order (Rom. 1:20) and also in man; in Christ, and in him alone, God's perfect likeness is to be seen. In verse 19 Paul extends the thought – 'in him, all the fullness (*plērōma*) of God was pleased to dwell'. In the comments on Ephesians 1:23 we have already noted the ambiguities inherent in the word *plērōma*. C. F. D. Moule's carefully argued conclusion is that 'Christ is thought of as containing, representing, all that God ıs'. We may not have the fully developed Christology of the fourth and fifth-century creeds, but there can be little doubt that Paul would echo the Johannine assertion that the man who has seen Christ has seen God, the Father.

It is this Christ who is described as the head of the body, the church (compare Eph. 1:22,23). Vincent Taylor comments, 'The name "the Head" asserts his inseparability from the church, but excludes his identity with it'. Comparison with v.24 where the church is thought of as 'the body of Christ' demonstrates the crucial importance of the concept. Christ does not only express the full character of God but is himself expressed through the total body of his disciples – the church. As head, he is both supreme in the body and also is its origin; Paul probably did not have ideas of control or direction in mind. This is borne out by the following phrases which should be understood in the context of the new creation, not the old. Beginning (*archē*, 18) is better translated as 'origin' – the church comes into being through his creative initiative, he is supreme among all. Of the English versions, the NEB perhaps best catches the sense of Paul's words. The universality of his supremacy is matched by the 'all things' of verse 20. The idea is not some vague universalism which excludes the necessity of repentance and faith, but rather the recognition that the benefits of Christ's death extend to the whole created order (compare Rom. 8:19-22; Isa. 11:6-9). He is indeed 'our peace' (Eph. 2:14) not only between Jew and Gentile, but between all created things.

1:21-23 The reconciliation of men

Paul now applies the principles of his Christology to the Colossian church. He has exalted Christ as the one through whom God chose to effect reconciliation between himself and the created order (20). What that reconciliation means for the Colossians is now spelt out. They who were estranged and alienated from God, opposed to him in their thinking and as a result doing things that were evil, are now reconciled. The intransitive use of the verb is perhaps deliberate – reconciliation is between God and his creation, and is also within the created order itself. The manuscripts vary greatly in the precise tense of the verb 'to reconcile'. Most versions, however, agree in the sense of the verse.

Reconciliation was effected 'in his body of flesh by his death' (22). The phrase probably distinguishes his earthly body from that of the church (compare v.18) but could also indicate the vital importance for Christian theology of the fact that Jesus really died. Many gnostic systems were to suggest that such a physical death was impossible for a divine being and only appeared to happen. Paul has no time for such a 'docetic' Christ. The consequence of Christ's death is that Christians can be presented before God as holy, blameless and irreproachable. The metaphor is that of a sacrifice acceptable to God. We become righteous by assimilation into the self-offering of Christ. Such an identification is essential to Paul's concept of reconciliation. It is, however, not without its demands. Any assurance which does not carry with it the necessity of faithful endurance can very easily become presumption. Temporary reconciliations are often worse than no reconciliation, so Paul reminds his readers that continuance in the faith is an essential mark of the genuine article. This is a frequent theme in the epistle.

The assertion that the gospel 'has been preached to every creature' (23) may seem puzzling. Paul probably means 'every type of' creature, i.e. in all the centres of civilisation, rather than 'all without exception'. This is an acceptable claim and one which accords with his own strategy as well as with Acts 1:8.

THOUGHT: Any assurance which does not carry with it the necessity of faithful endurance can very easily become presumption.

1:24-29 A minister of the church

Paul now turns in 1:24–2:3 to consider his own share in this reconciling work of God. He has already mentioned that he became a minister of the gospel (23); he now describes himself as a minister of the church (25). This is parallel to the thought in Ephesians 3:10 that the church is entrusted with the gospel and that in acting as an evangelist Paul is serving the church as well as the gospel.

Such service had led Paul into suffering; he writes in chains (4:18). This suffering, he argues, is a cause for joy not sorrow – a theme familiar from Philippians. But what does he mean by saying that he completes 'what is lacking in Christ's afflictions for the sake of his body'? Paul makes it quite clear elsewhere in the epistle that Christians have died and come to life with Christ (2:12-14). Therefore it does not mean that we complete Christ's sufferings as our contribution to our salvation, for they are sufficient in themselves. We are left with two alternatives. Either Paul means that individual Christians share in Christ's earthly sufferings through being 'in Christ', and that their share must be completed. Or, he means that the 'corporate Christ' must suffer before the purposes of God are complete. His own imprisonment is part of that total suffering and he therefore suffers on their behalf. Both ideas are consistent with Paul's thought, though the latter perhaps has more in its favour. C. F. D. Moule feels that the two should be combined. It is clear that Paul expected Christians to suffer, both personally and as a church, and that both are a result of being in Christ. Such suffering is part of God's plan and should therefore be welcomed.

Paul's service for the church involves 'fully proclaiming God's message' which he describes as 'the mystery hidden for ages and generations'. It is mysterious not because it is only revealed to the initiated, but because it comes by revelation, in this case the revelation of Christ's incarnation (compare 2:2 where Christ himself is identified with 'God's mystery'). This mystery has been revealed to the church (26) through the wealth of glory – of God's full character – revealed in the Incarnation and through Christ's presence, by his Holy Spirit, in the church. This in turn is the basis for their confidence 'in a glorious destiny to come' (27). No wonder therefore that Paul's full energies (29) combined with God's willing inspiration are directed to the goal of Christian maturity, a goal achieved by proclamation, warning and teaching (28).

2:1-3 Christ, the wisdom of God

Paul continues with the idea of hard work and effort as his thinking widens to include the Christian fellowship in the Lycus valley and all those who have never 'seen his face'. He strives in prayer, as v.2 shows, but 2 Cor. 11:28,29 also suggests that part of his effort comes from the weight of anxiety he feels as, even at a distance, he shares their 'growing pains'.

Paul's desires were always turned into prayer. So he prays first that their hearts and wills – the centre of their decision-making processes – may be encouraged. The thought is similar to that of 1:23 which highlighted the necessity of standing firm. Such encouragement comes from a deepening bond of love and the wealth of conviction arising from a growing insight and knowledge of Christ. God's mystery, again in the sense of something he alone can reveal, is here clearly identified with Christ, who is the embodiment of the wisdom and understanding of God. Paul's point here is that through an increasing knowledge of Christ they will enter more deeply into the wealth of God's own wisdom and understanding.

The description of Christ as possessing the wisdom and insight of God is an aspect of 1:19. Paul's reasons for singling it out are instructive. It was the claim of gnostics and their kind that they possessed a secret knowledge (hence their name) which explained the origin of evil and the means of salvation. Paul's insight into the person of Christ is now to be directed towards a refutation of that claim as well as a rejection of the practices of the heretics. Against that background he wishes to argue the sufficiency of Christ. The verse, therefore, neatly forms a bridge into his next major section (2:4–3:4).

Questions for further study and discussion on Colossians 1:1–2:3

1. On what is the Colossians' present love and faith based (5)? What does this phrase mean to you?

2. How important is it to present the gospel in terms of hope (compare 1:5,27)? How does our hope differ from the 'hopes' of the world around us?

3. It has been said of 1:9-11: 'This passage teaches us more about the essentials of prayer's requests than almost any other passage in the New Testament.' What can we learn of the aim of prayer, the ways this is to be achieved and its results? What do you find most challenging about this passage?

4. In verse 13 'the dominion of darkness' is contrasted with the 'kingdom of his Son'. Put into your own words the characteristics of the two kingdoms (see also 3:5-15). Why do you think so many people prefer the dominion of darkness?

5. 'I believe Christ is a good man whose example I want to follow, but that's all.' In the light of 1:15-20 what reply would you make to someone who said this?

6. Amongst the many questions raised today about the person of Christ, which do you feel are legitimate? How much help does Paul give us in our current debate?

7. What was the purpose of Christ's death (21-23)? The Colossians had many temptations to move away from the true faith. What temptations to move away from your first love are you faced with?

8. For what does Paul toil and strive (24-29)? Is this the corporate aim of your church? Should it be? Why? What part can you as individuals play in this?

9. In what ways does Paul, in prison, strive for the Colossians (2:1,2)? What encouragement is there here for elderly or housebound people?

2:4-7 Incorporation into Christ

This central section of the letter (2:4–3:4) is concerned directly with the Colossian heresy. Paul's argument is based on his assertion about Christ (3) and can be summarised as follows: because Christ contains all the wisdom of God, nobody is to deceive you into thinking that something extra is required. In him you have all that you need for life and salvation. Your incorporation into Christ, of which the drama of baptism speaks so strongly, involves you in a death and resurrection with him which is a decisive victory over the forces of evil. Therefore there is no need to submit to other regulations which imply that salvation is not complete in Christ.

Paul begins the section with a general exhortation to the Colossian Christians to continue in the way they had begun. His concern for their welfare is not lessened by his absence and he continues to rejoice in their firm stand in the faith (compare 1:23) as well as their 'well-ordered conduct'. Consequently he urges them to 'walk' (the Greek has 'walk' not 'live') 'in him' (6). This is a familiar Pauline metaphor. Their progress in the Christian life must be 'in Christ' – his must be the way they take and the atmosphere they breathe. They had received and trusted the tradition – the historical account of Jesus Christ – and in the same way they must continue to trust and live by incorporation into Christ. The Christian gospel is essentially an *historical* account of what happened in the past; yet also, essentially, it means incorporation *now* in the still living Person of whom it tells – 'the contemporary Christ' (C. F. D. Moule). So, changing the metaphor, they are to have their foundations in him and to be built up in him. Only then, by a continuous incorporation into Christ, will they become established in the faith and be able to give unlimited thanks to God.

THOUGHT: Your incorporation into Christ . . . involves you in a death and resurrection with him which is a decisive victory over the forces of evil.

2:8-15 Baptised into Christ's death

These verses form the central plank of Paul's argument and reason for rejecting the Colossian heretics (see Introduction, p. 70). His opening warning is not an attack against philosophy as such. It is an exhortation not to be led astray by speculations (NEB) which are a useless deceit because they do not lead to God. The so-called wisdom of his opponents is so much wind, based on man-made tradition (compare the true 'tradition' [6]) and 'elemental spirits'. This strange phrase either refers to the pagan idea of the 'elemental spirits which underlie the world' or to 'rudimentary and worldly notions'. Most commentators favour the former interpretation though both make good sense. Such human speculations are 'not according to Christ'. This is no caution against thinking; only against thinking in limited human terms without reference to God's revelation in Christ (8).

Paul's argument consists first of a repetition of his central doctrine of Christ (9, compare 1:19). If Christ embodies the fullness of God, then human speculations are unnecessary. The addition of bodily (*sōmatikos*) is interesting. It could simply be a simile for 'really' or 'in bodily form'. Both these interpretations stress the reality of the Incarnation and this is perhaps the natural way to interpret the phrase. Some have, however, suggested in the light of the Colossian situation that it could mean 'as an organised body', i.e. the totality of Godhead is not shared out (as in Gnosticism) through a hierarchy but is embodied in one 'organism' – in Christ; or it could mean 'in the body' (of Christ), i.e. the church.

Secondly, he lays down the significance of incorporation into Christ (10-12). It means *completeness* (10); because Christ possesses the fullness of the Godhead those incorporated 'in him' (the church) find their own fullness or fulfilment. Moreover, if the *plērōma* of God could dwell in a human frame how much more the *plērōma* of men. To suggest that such fulfilment or completeness could be found elsewhere, or by adding to Christ, is nonsense. It also means *death, burial and resurrection* (11,12). 'If it is asked *how* this "completeness", which has been brought within the human range by the Incarnation, is appropriated, the answer is that in Christian baptism (a rite deeper and greater than Jewish circumcision, whatever parallels may exist between the two) the believer is identified, by faith, with Christ in his obedient death and his triumphant resurrection' (C. F. D. Moule). The allusion to circumcision is probably made because it was one of the demands of the heretics. All right, says Paul, in your baptism (the opening verb of verse 12 is a participle 'having been baptised') you were circumcised by identification with Christ in the cutting off of his own flesh, i.e. in his death. Your baptism also involved a burial with Christ and through faith in God a resurrection to new life.

Sadly we shrink from Paul's bold use of language. We rightly stress that baptism is a sign, not the reality, yet we often fail to perceive that rightly used it effects the death and resurrection of which it speaks so eloquently. Its imagery is perhaps most clearly seen in some missionary situations today and in the past, where the village community gathered on one bank of the river, the church on the other. The candidate left the village, was baptised in the river and came out into the community of the church. Baptism is the universal equivalent of that local scene – we 'die' to the world and 'rise' to new life in Christ and his church.

This baptismal incorporation into Christ speaks of a reality which depends on what God has done in the death and resurrection of Christ (13,14). The Colossian Christians were uncircumcised, not only literally, for Paul is probably addressing Gentiles, but also spiritually. They were alienated from God. This has been reversed by God through their incorporation into Christ (13b). It was achieved through a process of forgiveness – he has cancelled the 'IOU' (14) with its legal obligation: 'I owe God obedience to his will. Signed, Mankind' (C. F. D. Moule). The obligation we had failed to keep he set aside – 'nailing it to the cross' (14). Christ nailed to the cross represents humanity's guilt. So we died with him and in our dying the IOU was cancelled. No one metaphor can ever exhaust the significance of the cross so Paul adds another (15). On the cross Christ won a victory over the forces which controlled the world – he led them as captives in his triumphal procession. If God in Christ crucified and raised to life again has done all that, then who dares to suggest a doctrine of 'Christ plus'?

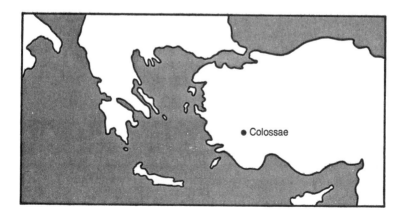

• Colossae

2:16-19 Unnecessary rituals

Paul's argument now turns to the detailed practices which the heretics said were necessary. If the powers controlling the physical world have been so clearly defeated by the death of Christ, there is no reason for submitting to mere physical and external rituals – they cannot add anything to the 'fullness' of incorporation into Christ, and their bases have been overthrown. From our standpoint it is difficult to know what precisely these people were advocating. It is clear that they considered the observance of various festivals, possibly Jewish, as essential, together with a strict diet (16). That such scruples were common is attested by passages like Romans 14:1-3; 1 Tim. 4:2,3; Hebrews 9:10; 13:9. Paul here describes them as a shadow (*skia*) of what is to come; the substance (*sōma*) being of Christ (17). The shadow/substance contrast was an integral part of Platonic philosophy; in addition the use of *sōma* – the body of Christ (the Greek has no verb) – would have direct associations with the church. The verse is therefore full of allusions which would be seen by different people in different lights. At this distance we can only say with certainty that Paul saw all these rituals – whether they were Jewish or pagan – as shadows; the reality was to be found in Christ; a truth he has already spelt out in terms of circumcision (11,12).

The practices alluded to in v.18 are even more obscure. 'Self-abasement' could well refer to fasting which fits the context well (23); the 'worship of angels' could either refer to the well-developed doctrine of angels in contemporary Judaism or the numerous 'demi-gods' of the Gnostic systems. Once again, Paul urges his readers not to allow themselves to be placed 'beyond the pale' by those who insist on these things. They base their teaching on visions and on materialistic and sensual thinking (18). The precise meaning of the original is not clear but the contrast between them and those 'who hold fast to the Head' – i.e. are firmly integrated into the body of Christ – could not be greater. The former are 'puffed up' with materialistic thinking; the latter are growing together as they work for their mutual benefit (compare Eph. 4:15,16).

2:20-23 Worldly life or Christian life

The final arrows of Paul's long argument against the false teachers of Colossae are contained in two conditional sentences. The first (2:20-23) expresses the negative implications of the gospel – 'if with Christ you died . . .'; the second (3:1-4) its positive aspirations – 'if you have been raised with Christ . . .'. In both cases the conditional clause arises from the theology Paul has already created (2:11-15). The 'ifs' are the 'ifs' of logic, not of doubt!

The negative argument is simply this. With Christ (by incorporation) you died to the elemental spirits (see on v. 8). You are no longer under their control, so do not go on behaving as if you were. If you submit to these false teachers and obey their petty regulations, then you are obeying human or worldly precepts and teaching (22). They may appear attractive and have gained a reputation for wisdom simply by virtue of their voluntary piety, fasting and asceticism – actions which always appear highly 'religious'. But they have no real value in checking sensuality. They do not deal with the root of the problem. The variations in the translation of v. 23 are the result of the fact that the 'verse is by consent regarded as hopelessly obscure – either owing to corruption or because we have lost the clue' (C. F. D. Moule). Perhaps the NEB has caught its flavour best.

TO THINK ABOUT: It is interesting to consider what are our modern equivalents of these worldly regulations. We perhaps do not live in an age of such obvious syncretism as Paul, at least not in terms of rules and regulations. The dangers, however, are still there, whether they take the form of Jewish celebrations, the legalism of total abstinence or the rituals of transcendental meditation.

3:1-4 Raised to life with Christ

The positive ambitions of Christian living stem from the fact that we have been raised with Christ (again by incorporation). The passive form of the verb is important, for the New Testament always stresses that God raised Christ from the dead. Paul, in describing our resurrection with or in him, makes the same point (for example 2:12). He is 'the raised Christ' rather than 'the risen Christ' and we are 'raised with him'. Such a resurrection is both past and future (1,4). By incorporation in Christ, we have been raised to life and must live accordingly. On the other hand, the full flowering of our life will only appear when he himself, who is our life, appears in glory.

Paul's command is double-edged – 'You have been raised with Christ, then both *seek* the things that are above and *set your minds* on them.' The first verb suggests a quest or enquiry; the second implies the fixed basis of all our thinking. Both our aspirations and our thoughts must be centred not 'on the earth' but 'above'.

The nature of the 'things that are above' (1,2) is best understood in contrast to the false teachers whose minds are set on materialistic and sensual thinking (2:18). Their thinking is bounded by the material world and its pleasures. In contrast, the Christian's horizons are totally different. His mind is fixed on the reality of the heavenly world and its standards. Such a man does not, however, ignore or despise the physical, created order. He sees it in a new divine perspective. His ambitions and aspirations are viewed from the standpoint of the eternal order, not its temporary 'shadow'. This applies not only to our thinking, but to our very life (3). Just as the treasures of God's wisdom are hid in Christ (2:3) so also is our life. Our new life as members of the church is intimately connected with his own. His final appearance in glory will therefore be ours as well, for he 'is our life'.

CHALLENGE: Both our aspirations and our thoughts must be centred not 'on the earth' but 'above'.

3:5-11 Dying to the old

Again Paul considers the negative (5-11) and positive (12-17) aspects of the Christian's life this time in terms of practical Christian living. Most of Paul's letters fall into two parts – the first doctrinal, the second practical. The divisions are never rigid, however, because his instructions about daily life usually arise naturally from his theology. In addition, his theology always has a clear ethical content and vice versa. Incorporation into Christ which we have seen to be the central theme of this letter can never be a merely intellectual exercise; it involves the whole person. So 'you have died with Christ . . .' (2:20) leads naturally into 'Put to death, therefore . . .' (3:5). This latter has its parallel in 3:9,10. This 'reclothing' is the Christian's way of expressing his involvement in Christ's death and resurrection (compare 2:11,12; 3:3,4).

The vices which are to be crucified concern first 'the use of our limbs for sensual purposes' (5). Certainly the list which follows is consistent with this understanding (for discussion of their meaning see on Eph. 5:3-7). Again Paul identifies covetousness with idolatry. If we desire something too much we make it an idol – it has become the object of our worship. It is strange that 'the wrath (*orgē*) of God' (6) should be described before the injunction of verse 8: 'put away anger (*orgē*), wrath (*thumos*)'. C. H. Dodd argued that the phrase should be understood as the principle of retribution which is inherent in the universe. A better solution is probably to be found in the realisation that we can only speak of God by analogy – he is like this particular human conception. His 'anger' is *like* human anger, but it is clear from his character revealed elsewhere that it differs in involving no vindictiveness or personal hatred. He is 'angry' with the sinner, but still 'loves' him!

Secondly, the list in vs.8,9 moves into areas of speech. What we say is as important as what we do, and its control is as difficult, if not harder than that of our limbs and organs. Such control is part of 'the new nature', or literally 'man'. This is not just an individual condition. Our 'reclothing' is corporate (compare the 'new man' of Eph. 2:15). Paul is not simply arguing for an 'individual change of character but . . . a corporate recreation of humanity' (C. F. D. Moule). It is, then, this new corporate personality which is being gradually developed in the life of the church (10) 'after the image of its creator', i.e. Christ (compare 1:18-20). This corporate understanding makes good sense of v.11, which otherwise could appear intrusive. One of the qualities of the new humanity is that it transcends all distinctions of race, culture, and sex (compare Gal. 3:28). In Christ all such divisions disappear because all become one corporate personality.

3:12-17 Rising to the new

Paul's description of his readers, 'God's chosen, holy and beloved,' is taken straight from the language of the old Covenant (compare Isa. 43,44). All these words were used to describe 'Israel after the flesh'; they now describe 'the new Israel'. They stress that the church depends on God's initiative and undeserved love. Therefore Christians must display a corresponding character. So Paul lists the qualities which must replace those they have shed. Many of them are clear opposites of the bitternesses and divisions contained in the former list; none is easy to observe to the full. Once again (compare Eph. 4:32) the standard is that of God himself displayed in the forgiveness granted through Jesus Christ. The garment which covers them all is love (*agapē*). The RSV has paraphrased its description, which in the Greek reads 'which is the binding together of completeness (or perfection)'. The NEB seems to be a better reading. Paul's thought is that love both holds everything together – it gives coherence – and, in doing so, completes or fulfils everything.

The peace of God is said to be (or should be) the 'umpire' in our hearts. This is another image borrowed from the games. A similar word occurs in 2:18 (*katababreuō*, here *babreuō*) which the RSV translates as 'disqualify'. The picture is of the one who presides over the games. So the peace which comes from obedience to Christ must preside over our conflicts of will and conscience, 'bringing co-ordination and direction to life' (C. F. D. Moule). By becoming, as Christians, members of one body, we are called to that peace. Gratitude (15) is also an essential accompaniment.

Verse 16 offers a number of possible translations as well as a number of interesting thoughts. The RSV has solved one problem by taking 'singing' before 'psalms and spiritual songs'. A more literal translation would suggest we are 'to teach and admonish each other with psalms and hymns and spiritual songs, in gratitude singing in our hearts to God' (compare Eph. 5:19). Whichever reading is right, a number of points are clear. First, there is the importance of allowing the gospel to shape our minds and wills. Secondly, the mutual responsibility we have for teaching and admonishing (correcting) each other. Love is vital in the latter exercise. Thirdly, the great importance of praise and gratitude in the Christian life. Finally, everything is to be done in the name of the Lord Jesus and in an attitude of thanksgiving (17, compare 1 Cor. 10:31). The phrase implies both 'on his behalf,' and 'consistently with his character'.

Questions for further study and discussion on Colossians 2:4–3:17

1. The Colossians were told that there were extra ceremonies and regulations which they must fulfil for a full knowledge of Christ (2:16-23). What extra experiences and practices are we sometimes told we must have in order to be 'real Christians'? What is our answer?

2. Chapter 2:6 demands that our whole lives be 'lived in the conscious presence of Christ'. How can we try to achieve this (3:1-4)?

3. What two images are used in 2:7? What do these teach about the Christian life?

4. What modern parallels can you see to the attitudes and practices Paul is combating in 2:16-23? How are they affecting the life of the church?

5. How would someone who is seeking to follow Paul's command in 3:1-4 answer the charge, 'He is so heavenly minded he is no earthly use'?

6. If Paul were writing 3:11 today, what might he mention? There are real cultural and emotional differences between groups of people: to what extent, and how, do we take these into account?

7. Where you work 'earthly passions' may be rampant. When you strike the death blow to these in yourself, how do people react? What do they find most disturbing and challenging?

8. Can you give examples of the way covetousness is idolatry (5)?

9. Chapter 3:12-17 contains a list of characteristics of the Christian community. Which do you find most difficult to practise?

3:18-21 Family relationships

These verses are a shortened form of those in Ephesians 5:22–6:9 (see page 37-9). The fact that Ephesians presents the fuller version may indicate that Colossians was written first but this is not conclusive. The differences are interesting. First, the wife's 'subjection' is said to be 'fitting in the Lord' rather than 'as to the Lord' (Eph. 5:22). It implies that it is the right thing for those incorporated into the Christian community. Secondly, husbands are not to 'be harsh' with their wives. It is the negative side of the coin. Ephesians speaks positively of love and care. The word conjures up pictures of an embittered husband taking it out on his wife.

Children and fathers are commanded to behave, on the one hand, with obedience – an attitude which is not only right (Eph. 6:1) but which, in an explanation of that phrase, is said to please the Lord – and, on the other hand, without provocation. Such sensitive understanding of children and the realisation that excessive provocation and harsh treatment can lead to discouragement is an important part of family relationships in Christ.

3:22-4:1 Slaves and masters

It is clear from 4:9 that Colossians and Philemon were written together. In all probability, then, Paul had Onesimus near him as he wrote these words. Again their substance is essentially that of Ephesians 6:5-9, but in this case we can take Philemon as the practical outworking of 4:1. That letter is really the best commentary on Paul's thinking about the master/slave relationship and should be read with these verses.

The language of reward and punishment is, perhaps, stronger here than in Ephesians 6:8 where the idea is of a 'tit for tat', or *quid pro quo*. Here the reward is spoken of in terms of 'the inheritance' (24). This is not meant to be understood in a mercenary way. It means, rather, that life in the kingdom of God is reserved for those who display its qualities here on earth, not for those who don't (25), for they, by their wrongdoing, voluntarily shut themselves out from God's presence.

4:2-6 Final instructions

These verses consist of a series of admonitions which do not have any necessary connection with each other. They are Paul's final instructions to the church before his concluding greetings.

On two occasions the disciples fell asleep while Jesus was praying – at the Transfiguration (Luke 9:32) and in Gethsemane (Matt. 26:40,41). Paul is obviously aware of similar temptations, so he enjoins them not only to persist in their prayer but to be awake in doing so. He is not perhaps thinking of physical sleep on this occasion so much as the danger of praying automatically or casually. True prayer should always be accompanied by thanksgiving (compare Phil. 4:6 and Paul's own example, for instance 1:3-14). He makes one specific request for himself (compare Eph. 6:19), and those with him: clarity and opportunity in preaching the gospel. With a delightful metaphor he asks for 'a door for the word'; what we would call 'an opening'. His request for such a door is so that he may declare 'the mystery of Christ', a contraction of his thought in 1:26,27. With that in mind he asks for prayer that he may give it 'a public display' (4). This is his solemn responsibility as a minister of the gospel, even though it has placed him in prison.

Our attitude to non-Christians should be tactful, we should make the most of every opportunity. The thought is similar to that in Ephesians 5:15,16. Paul is conscious that our conduct often speaks as loudly as our words and that opportunities are given for honouring Christ even if we do not say anything about him.

Finally our speech must be 'seasoned with salt' – 'never insipid' (NEB). It is difficult to know precisely what Paul meant by this metaphor. Salt – potash from the Dead Sea – was used as a fertiliser and a purifier in the ancient world as well as a preservative. It might therefore speak of wholesome or fruitful speech. 'If a Christian is ever difficult company, it ought to be because he demands too much, not too little, from his fellows' responsiveness and wit' (C. F. D. Moule).

TO THINK OVER: Examine your contacts and the things you have said to them in the light of Paul's statement.

4:7-9 Tychicus and Onesimus

Paul sent his letters, Ephesians, Colossians and Philemon, to the churches with Tychicus and Onesimus. The former we have met before in Ephesians 6:21,22. As we saw there he came from Asia Minor (Acts 20:4) and 2 Timothy confirms that he was sent to Ephesus either with this letter or possibly another. He appears to have been considered as a possible relief for Titus in Crete (Tit. 3:12). All these references confirm his loyalty and usefulness to Paul. He was sent so that the Christians of the Lycus valley might hear at first hand how Paul was (7, compare 9).

Onesimus was a runaway slave belonging to Philemon in whose house (Philemon 2) the church apparently met. He met Paul in prison, was converted (Philemon 10), and became a trusted and well-loved brother. His name meant 'useful' and Paul with a characteristic pun writes to Philemon about him as 'once so little use to you, now useful indeed' (Philemon 11). In fact Paul expresses the wish to keep him but feels it is his duty to return him to his master. So he wrote to Philemon in order to persuade him to receive Onesimus not as a slave, but as a brother. The comment of Aristeides is again pertinent, 'as for their servants . . . they persuade them to become Christians for the love that they have towards them; and when they have become so, they call them without distinction brethren' (*Apology*, c. AD 150).

4:10-14 Other friends

Paul conveys greetings from a number of people who were presumably known to the Christians of the Lycus valley. Aristarchus is mentioned in Acts 19:29; 20:4; 27:2 and there is no reason to doubt that the same person is in mind in all these references. He probably came from Thessalonica and shared Paul's last missionary journey to Rome. Whether he was literally a prisoner is not clear. He could have voluntarily stayed with Paul in his confinement (compare Philemon 23). One cannot help wondering what the instructions about Mark were! Perhaps, because he had caused a rift between Paul and Barnabas (Acts 13:13; 15:37-39), he was ostracised by the churches and Paul wished to reinstate him. Anyway, his inclusion here shows that Paul now valued him. Of Jesus Justus we know nothing except that, like the other two, he was a Jewish Christian.

Epaphras is again mentioned (see on 1:7), with the added comment that he continues to pray earnestly for them. It is often the lot of an evangelist that he has to leave his converts to develop without his help. Both Epaphras and Paul had learnt the value of prayer in that circumstance. Epaphras' prayer is for stable maturity and that they may be convinced of God's will. Paul also commends him for his hard work for the other towns of the valley, probably in both prayer and preaching.

Luke and Demas are familiar names. The former was constantly at Paul's side from the time of the second missionary journey. He not only placed his medical skill at Paul's disposal but also recorded the account of the gospel and of the establishment of the churches for our benefit. Demas is a sadder figure. He is not commended here, and in 2 Tim. 4:10 he is said to have 'left Paul in the lurch'. Not a welcome epitaph.

4:15-18 Final greetings

The link with Laodicea is interesting. We do not know Paul's letter to Laodicea, unless it is what we call Ephesians, which has no destination in most manuscripts. Probably the simplest explanation is right: that it has been lost. Whatever the right answer to the riddle it is clear that there was considerable communication between the two places and that Paul anticipates a wide circulation for his writing.

Archippus is addressed in Philemon together with Philemon and Apphia. He may have been their son (so A. F. Walls suggests in *The New Bible Dictionary*). The Colossian references may imply that he was called to be an elder or to have a particular ministry to the church at Laodicea. We will probably never know for certain, but the message is clear. Whatever his ministry was he was to fulfil it. That is all that is required of us: that we carry out to the full the job that God has entrusted to us.

Paul's final comment and greeting is deeply moving. Presumably he dictated the epistle and added the final greeting in his own hand. It is the characteristic Christian note of 'grace'.

Questions for further study and discussion on Colossians 3:18-4:18

1. What are the 'timeless principles' which Paul sets out for marriage (3:18,19, compare Eph. 5:21-32). What would you say are the most important factors for a successful marriage?

2. The standards Paul set for relationships in the household were a radical departure from contemporary practice. What should be the distinctive marks of Christian family life today?

3. What command does Paul give to parents? What is your aim for your children? How can you achieve this?

4. The command to honour one's parents is lifelong. What difficulties arise when one's parents are elderly – and what new privileges and joys come?

5. Using 3:18–4:1 and any other passages you can think of, try to state what you believe to be the Christian view of work.

6. In 4:2, why do you think Paul added the words 'being watchful'? What do you find you have to watch against when you pray? How do you do this?

7. In the light of 4:2-4 how should we be praying for each other? What particular requests would you make in order better to fulfil your own ministry?

8. Why do you think we so often waste opportunities (4:5)?

9. Chapter 4:6 is a warning against being boring and boorish. How can we avoid this?

10. Paul never failed to give commendation where it was deserved. How do you treat your fellow-labourers in the gospel?

Introduction

Paul was in Thessalonica for a relatively short time (Acts 17:1-10) before leaving hurriedly for Beroea. Even there he was hustled on by the Jews of Thessalonica. Since he had only preached for three weeks in Thessalonica Paul was obviously concerned to know how the church was developing, especially as persecution was assured. So when he reached Athens he sent Timothy back to find out (1 Thess. 3:1,2). Timothy then returned to Paul in Corinth (Acts 18:5) bringing good news but reporting that there were a number of problems. The major doctrinal issue concerned the second coming. Some thought its imminence meant they should stop work (1 Thess. 4:11; 2 Thess. 3:6,11); others were worried about those who had already died (1 Thess. 4:13-17). They were also interested in the signs of the end (1 Thess. 5 and 2 Thess. 2). In all these matters Paul is at pains to avoid speculation, to stress the moral imperative of the second coming and to balance the extreme teaching that was circulating. The other problems appear to have been the danger of immorality (1 Thess. 4:3-8), criticism of Paul (1 Thess. 2:5-11) and possibly division in the church (1 Thess. 4:9; 5:12,13). Paul's remarks, however, are mainly complimentary.

All the circumstances point to these letters being the earliest that Paul wrote. Both letters appear to have been written about the same time. Perhaps the second was occasioned by a further report suggesting that there was still trouble over the question of the second coming. In both we see Paul the pastor at work, caring for his flock.

New Testament teaching on the coming of Christ in the light of modern study is thoroughly covered by Dr Colin Brown in the *New International Dictionary of New Testament Theology* Vol. 2, pp. 901-931, The Parousia and Eschatology in the New Testament. As well as providing a full survey of both modern theological and New Testament study he gives a number of illuminating insights into the thinking of all the New Testament writers on the subject.

1 Thessalonians: Contents

2 Thessalonians: Contents

1:1-3 Remembering with thanks

The letter comes from Paul, Silvanus (presumably Silas in its Latin form) and Timothy but it is quite clear as the letter develops that the main driving force is Paul. He writes to 'the church of the Thessalonians'; elsewhere he writes, for example, to 'the church of God at Corinth'. The most similar ascription to that in Thessalonians occurs in Galatians where he writes to 'the churches of Galatia'. The word *ecclēsia* can be used both for the world-wide church of God and a local congregation. It is deliberately ambiguous, for the local congregation is the expression of the total church – it is 'The church of God in Corinth or Thessalonica . . .'. Its use here to refer to the local church is perhaps an indication that Paul was not intending the letter for wider circulation, unlike Ephesians or Colossians. The church is described as 'in God the Father and the Lord Jesus Christ'. This unusual phrase is perhaps in order to remind the Thessalonians that Christianity was not different from Judaism but was its fulfilment. It was from the Jews that the opposition at Thessalonica came.

This opening chapter is filled with all the good things that Paul has heard about the church. It is not a piece of flattery but a frank acknowledgement of the work of God in their lives. It is natural therefore that he should begin with thanksgiving for their faith, love and hope – the familiar Christian trilogy. The three qualities do not stand alone – 'your work of faith, and labour of love and steadfastness of hope'. The NEB and GNB have better expressed the point by reversing the order of the words – 'how your faith has shown itself in action, your love in labour, and your hope . . . in fortitude'. Faith should issue in work (*ergon*), love in labour (*kopos* – a word implying toil and strain; perhaps here it is simply used as a variant for *ergon*) and hope in Jesus Christ should bring patience or fortitude in the face of persecution. All this had come true in Thessalonica.

1:4-10 The word and the Spirit

What had brought about these things for which Paul gives thanks? Paul sums it up in one sentence (9,10). They had received Paul, Silas and Timothy and they had 'turned to God from idols, to serve the living and true God and to wait for his Son from heaven, whom he raised from the dead, Jesus who delivers us from the wrath to come'. In short, they were converted. First, it involved a *turning from* the worship of idols, in their case quite literally, and a *turning to* God. In so doing they acknowledged that he alone was 'living and true' and worthy of their service. Secondly, it gave them a hope – they awaited the return of Christ – a return which would mean their deliverance from God's judgement, and which was possible because God had raised Christ from the dead.

This conversion came as a result of three things: the gospel faithfully and convincingly proclaimed, the power of the Spirit and the example of Paul and his companions (5). There was nothing half-hearted about Paul's presentation of the gospel – it was preached with conviction, and in the power of the Spirit. The word of God is no empty word – it is, says Paul elsewhere (1 Cor. 1:18) 'the power of God'. But word and Spirit were also demonstrated in the lives of Paul and his companions. What they said rang true and convinced the Thessalonians because they could see the gospel in action. The preacher of God's word should always be an embodiment of the truth he proclaims.

The result was that the Thessalonians began to do the same thing (6-8): they received the word and suffered for it. But the suffering was outweighed by their joy in the Holy Spirit, so that they in turn became an example, a pattern, to all in Macedonian and Achaia. So effective was their example that Paul did not even have to preach (8). They had 'trumpeted' the word of God by their speech and by their lives. Here is the power of God – in his word, his Spirit and his people, 'chosen and beloved' (4), the people of his new covenant.

2:1-8 Seeking God's approval

Evidently Paul's opponents had been working hard in Thessalonica and had attributed all sorts of bad motives and methods to the missionaries. So Paul defends his behaviour, not in order to vindicate himself, but because he saw such comments as an attack on the gospel itself. Their 'visit' (the word is *eisodos,* translated as 'welcome' in 1:9) was not in vain, because even though they had been thrown into prison at Philippi (Acts 16) they still had the courage to preach elsewhere in Macedonia. Their courage, like the gospel itself, was God-given (4,2).

The accusations against them seem to be that they were preaching 'error', practising 'uncleanness' and catching their converts by guile (3). Amongst the methods which came under the last category were flattery and disguised greed (5). Instead of these base motives, says Paul, they had the single desire to please God who had entrusted them with the gospel itself. Any suggestion that they were preaching to please men was therefore ruled out. They could indeed have used their God-given status as apostles to 'throw their weight about' (6b) but they didn't. Instead they treated the Thessalonians as a nurse treats a child. Some manuscripts read 'babes' instead of 'gentle' (*nēpioi* instead of *ēpioi,* since the last letter of the preceding word is 'n' it is easy to see how the error crept in). 'Gentle' clearly makes better sense, even though many of the older manuscripts have 'babes'. Paul insists that they behaved in a genuinely affectionate manner towards the Thessalonians, so much so that they shared themselves as well as the gospel (8). It is very easy for a Christian minister or leader to become too professional, to 'deliver the goods' and leave it there. True Christian ministry involves the giving of oneself as Christ gave himself on the cross.

2:9-12 Impeccable behaviour

One of the rights of an apostle or minister of the gospel was that he could live at the expense of the people to whom he went (1 Cor. 9:4). We know Paul was a tent-maker (Acts 18:3), though he does not say here that he practised the trade in Thessalonica. Nevertheless he and his companions 'worked night and day' so that they would not be a burden to their converts. So important was his message that Paul was prepared to work himself to the bone in order to provide enough to support himself; then he could preach the gospel 'free of charge'.

As he defends himself before these accusations of deceit and greed, he calls both God and his converts into the witness box. Both, he says, can testify to his behaviour – it was *holy*, fit for God, *righteous*, it conformed to God's standard, and *blameless*, it gave no cause for rebuke. If the nurse is characterised by her tenderness (7), the father is known for his encouragement. So Paul says that like a father they exhorted, encouraged and charged the Thessalonians in order that they would lead lives worthy of God himself. The gospel call is 'into his own kingdom and glory'. We must therefore display the standards of the kingdom and the character of the King. God's kingdom and glory were central to the message of Jesus; he came 'preaching the good news of the kingdom'. This is no earthly or physical realm, but is to be found whenever men acknowledge and accept God's rule. The 'glory' of God was seen both in the transfiguration, and also on the cross (John 17, compare the conversation about Christ's death during the transfiguration [Luke 9:30]). It is the revelation of the full character of God.

Our calling is to enter that kingdom and to share that glory.

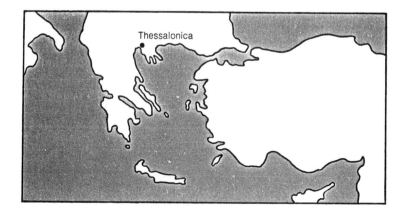
Thessalonica

2:13-16 The word of God

The final plank in Paul's defence against those who accused him and his companions of false motives and methods concerns the Thessalonians themselves. They had accepted the gospel as the true word of God. Of the two words used – 'receive' and 'accept' – the second conveys the idea of welcome, being the word often used for receiving a guest. No wonder Paul gives thanks. Such should be the response to all true preaching: to forget the preacher in the joy of receiving the word of God himself. Only this can bring the transformation Paul has already noticed (1:3).

The result of this 'welcome' was that they became 'imitators of the churches of God in Judea' (14), not this time in the sense that they followed their example (compare 1:6), although the word is the same, but that they suffered the same fate (compare Acts 8:1). Their fellow-countrymen, the Macedonians, persecuted them in the same way that the Jews had persecuted the Christians of Judea. Paul's list of accusations against his own people makes bitter reading. They killed the Lord, Jesus the man of Nazareth, as they had already killed the prophets. Paul's words are the plain statement of Christ's message in the parable of the husbandmen (Matt. 21:33-43). The Jews also rejected the Christians, initially regarded as a sect within Judaism (for example study the use of the title 'the Way' in Acts 9:2; 19:9,23; 22:4; 24:14,22). They incurred God's displeasure and opposed the best interests of mankind by preventing the preaching of the gospel to the Gentiles. 'I fear', translates J. B. Phillips, 'they are completing the full tale of their sins' (16).

The history of Jewish-Christian relations has not been helped by the accusation that the Jews were responsible for the death of Jesus. Recent Jewish writers have pointed out that the Romans actually condemned Jesus to death, even though it was the Jews who had brought him to trial. Paul's strong language must be understood as the deep-seated feelings of one who was himself a Jew, and felt very bitterly the failure of his people to recognise in Christ the fulfilment of all that Judaism stood for. For him Judaism lived on in the new Israel. He was not the first member of the race to castigate his fellow Jews with harsh and bitter words. The prophets did so and were equally rejected by the Jews of their day. The persecution of 'the nation which crucified Jesus', as the Crusaders called the Jews, is a sad blot on Christian history. Paul longed for their conversion (Romans 10:1) not their destruction. Certainly, a minority of Jews of Jesus' day must bear some of the blame for his death, but all mankind is involved. We are all to blame by association and attitude.

Gordon Jessup's book *No strange God* (Olive Press, 1976) provides an invaluable introduction to modern Judaism as well as giving a useful, if brief, comment on Christian-Jewish relations.

Questions for further study and discussion on 1 Thessalonians 1:1–2:16

1. Commenting on a new play, the actress Billie Whitelaw once said, 'I feel that this is the stuff of everyone's life: how to get through the day, to keep hopelessness out.' How do you react? Is that the 'stuff of everyone's life'? What prevented the Thessalonians' labour from being drudgery, their struggles from being unbearable (1:3,4)? Discuss how this can be true in our own lives.

2. In what had the Thessalonians imitated Paul (1:6-10)? When is it good to imitate others, and when is imitation harmful? (Compare Martin Buber who dreamt he had died and was before God, who said, 'I don't condemn you for not being Moses, but for not being Martin Buber.')

3. How does Paul sum up the conversion experience of the Thessalonians (1:9,10)? How would you, in one sentence, sum up your own conversion experience? What were the idols of your life?

4. In his ministry Paul contrasts living to get and living to give. What does he say he could have grasped for himself, and instead what does he give (2:4-11)? What underhand methods are Christian workers tempted to use today? How do we guard against them?

5. To live to please men is an ever present temptation. In what ways do you experience it? How can we fight against it?

6. It is easy to be influenced by malicious gossip which is disguised as godly advice. How do you set about assessing such advice?

7. 'We must display the standards of the kingdom and the character of the King' (page 100). How does Paul do this in 1:1–2:12?

8. The Jews were hated in the ancient world because of their arrogance. They knew they were chosen but thought they were chosen for privilege. Does anti-semitism persist today in England or elsewhere? Why do you think this is? What can we do about it? And what about other forms of racism?

2:17-20 Paul's joy and glory

Paul now turns in 2:17–3:13 to an account of his own relationship with the Thessalonians. He explains how and why he sent Timothy to them (3:2) and describes Timothy's report (3:6-8), a report which drove him to thanksgiving (3:9) and prayer (3:10-13).

With deliberate emphasis – on the 'we' (17) and the 'I, Paul' (18) – Paul stresses his desire to return to Thessalonica. Having left in a hurry (see Introduction p. 95) he earnestly wishes to return and see how the young church has fared. There was, after all, only a limited amount that even Paul could teach them in three weeks! He describes himself and his companions as 'bereft . . . in person, not in heart'. His affection was still with them but he longed to see them face to face. Paul's inability to return is unequivocally attributed to Satan. Perhaps their readers would understand the allusion, but at this distance there is no obvious reason why Paul and his companions were prevented from paying the Thessalonians a visit, unless it was the inevitable imprisonment that would follow.

The reason for wanting to return so badly is that Paul looks upon the Thessalonians as his 'hope or joy or crown of boasting' before God and 'his joy and glory'. Paul views them in this light in the context of the coming of Jesus Christ. The word used is *parousia*, which appears here for the first time in Christian literature. Its literal meaning is 'presence' but it quickly came to be a technical term for the return of Jesus Christ. Paul's thought is that when Christ returns he, and his companions, will be able to point to the Thessalonians as their 'victor's laurel' – proof that they had faithfully run the race and carried out their commission.

QUESTION: To what will we be able to point as proof that we have faithfully run the race and carried out our commission?

3:1-5 Timothy's mission

As well as being aware of the benefit of suffering to the church (Phil. 1:12-14), Paul was acutely aware of the temptation to give in under duress. The danger to a young struggling church could be very great. So, knowing that persecution was inevitable in Thessalonica after what he had suffered there, Paul is doubly concerned for their welfare (5), a concern shared by his companions (1). He had laboured hard (*kopos* [5] – implying toil and effort) in preaching and teaching and he is anxious lest the temptation to give way has proved too strong and brought his efforts to nothing.

So when they could no longer bear the anguish caused by uncertainty and concern, they sent Timothy. The purpose of his journey was twofold. First, it was to discover how the converts were (5): Paul wished 'to know their faith' – had they survived? It was a mission of inquiry. But secondly, and perhaps of more importance, it was a mission of encouragement (2,3). Paul can scarcely have had any time to teach them more than the bare rudiments of the faith, so Timothy's commission was 'to establish them in their faith'. He was to strengthen their faith and to exhort them to stand firm. There is no encouragement like that of fellow-Christians when we are tempted to 'move' away from our faith.

Paul offers them no respite from persecution, however. He recognises that this 'is to be our lot' (3). Affliction is a necessary part of the Christian life. 'In the world you have tribulation,' said Jesus (John 16:33) and that was not an isolated saying. He repeatedly warned his disciples of what was to come. Today, in a country where such open persecution is unusual, if not unknown, it is easy to be complacent. If we lived in Moslem lands, for example, we would be only too aware of the truth of Paul's words. Even in the Western world affliction can be, and is, still present. If our faith causes us no suffering, perhaps we are not really working it out in our daily community life.

3:6-10 Timothy's report

History has been foreshortened in Paul's account. We know nothing of Timothy's visit or how long it lasted. All we are told is that his report filled Paul and Silas with great joy and thanksgiving. The change of mood between vs. 5 and 6 is very marked, 'But now . . .'. Paul begins (6) by recounting Timothy's report, which he describes as 'having evangelised us' (the Greek verb is used elsewhere in the New Testament for preaching the gospel itself). Paul and Silvanus heard of their faith, their trust in God, and their love (*agapē*, the uniquely Christian love). In 1:3 Paul adds their hope which has bred patience. Timothy also told of their continuing affection for Paul and his companions – they had not disowned their spiritual parents. This report brought such great reassurance and joy that Paul breaks off in the middle of the sentence to tell of his happiness.

The report has brought Paul 'comfort' (7) – the verb is the same as in verse 2 (where the RSV translates it as 'exhort'). It is comfort in the old English sense of 'strengthen' or 'encourage'. Their faith has provided great reassurance in difficult times – in Corinth Paul was undergoing distress and affliction (both words, *anankē* and *thlipsis*, speak of strong outwaard pressure). In fact he now 'lives' (8) because of their firm stand for Christ. It is a vivid image, reflecting Paul's conviction that the whole body of Christ is radically affected if one part suffers, or, even worse, is amputated (compare 1 Cor. 12:26). Their failure would have been the death of part of himself. His rejoicing (9,10) is the opposite side of the same coin. It is expressed in his fine rhetorical question, 'What thanksgiving can we render to God for you, for all the joy which we feel for your sake . . .?' Not that they had nothing else to learn – he still wishes to return and 'supply what is lacking in their faith' (10). There is always more to learn in the Christian life. We all need the wisdom and insight of those who are ahead of us in their understanding of the faith.

3:11-13 Spontaneous prayer

Paul's final words in this section are a spontaneous prayer arising from the encouragement Timothy has brought. Characteristically he turns his longings for the Thessalonians into prayer and commits himself, his companions and the church itself to God's care and control.

His first request concerns himself and his two companions. He prays that God himself 'and our Lord Jesus' may guide or make straight the way to Thessalonica. In the light of 2:18 his prayer is to be understood as a request for the removal of whatever obstacles had been placed in his way. The close association of God the Father and Jesus Christ as the one to whom the request is made is an early indication that the Christians had little hesitation in addressing prayer to Jesus. It is also an indication of his divinity – only God could be addressed in prayer – and of his oneness with the Father.

His second request is for the church in Thessalonica. It is for an increase in love. The two verbs – increase and abound – are virtually synonymous. Paul wishes their love to go on increasing in ever greater measure. Christian love is both for each other and for all men. As Jesus pointed out in the parable of the Good Samaritan, love for our neighbour does not stop at those who share our beliefs, or those to whom we are naturally drawn, but extends to all who need it. When such love reaches its full flowering, the Thessalonians' lives will be established as 'unblameable in holiness' before God. Again, the two words 'unblameable' and 'holiness' are very similar in meaning. Paul prays that when Christ appears at his *'parousia'* they may be found fully fit for God in common with all who are 'the saints' (13), who are set apart for God. The supreme importance of this love is expressed in Col. 3:14 where it is said to hold together and to complete all the other virtues (see p. 87).

4:1-8 Sanctification, the will of God

Paul now turns from a consideration of what has happened in the past to deal with the particular problems which faced the church in Thessalonica, as well as with more general instructions about Christian living. These first eight verses contain a call to holiness of life. It is clearly a repetition of the basic Christian teaching which had accompanied the preaching of the gospel (2). Paul reminds the Thessalonians of these moral standards for two reasons. First, they lived amidst the immorality of the Greek world where chastity was of no importance, so there must have been an ever-present danger of a lapse in these matters. In that, our own world is not so very different. They, and we, need to have these standards placed continually before our eyes. Secondly, Paul has a more subtle reason for repeating these lists. Twice (3,7) he reminds his readers that God has called them to holiness. We all know this only too well; the problem is to live it out in practice. Paul is aware of that, that there is no 'secret', no solution which makes holy living simple for the Christian. All he can do is remind us of two things: the standards God requires (3-6) and the gift of his Holy Spirit (8), who co-operates with us by living God's life in us. We are not alone in our struggle, but the responsibility for our behaviour still lies with us.

The vices and virtues which are singled out are concerned with sexual matters. Immorality (*porneia* – v.3) serves as a title for what follows. Instead of behaving immorally, the Thessalonians are 'to possess or acquire their vessel in holiness and honour'. This strange phrase could mean 'control your own body' (so NEB, GNB mg) or it could be a way of saying 'treat your wife well' (compare RSV, GNB). This latter interpretation has the support of Augustine, amongst others. Neither interpretation is completely satisfactory. The gist of Paul's argument is, however, clear. In matters of sexuality our behaviour is not to be governed by uncontrolled lust (5); by such behaviour we take advantage of our brother man (or woman, by implication), and rightly incur God's judgement. Because holiness is *God's* demand, immorality is not just a social evil, but a sin against God himself (8).

CHALLENGE: We are not alone in our struggle, but the responsibility for our behaviour still lies with us.

4:9-12 Increasing love

Paul has already commended the Thessalonians for their 'love which has shown itself in labour' (1:3, NEB) and prayed that it may increase and abound (3:12). Although they need no further teaching on the matter (9) and are practising what they have learnt (10), there must always be the danger of complacency. So he exhorts them to go on loving more and more. The verb is exactly the same as in 3:12. There he *prays* that they may 'abound' in love and here he *urges* them to abound more in love. Prayer and exhortation are a powerful force. It is easy to use one and not the other and think we have discharged our Christian duty. Our prayers need always to be appropriately followed up in active Christian work which needs to be supported by prayer. Paul used two words for love in these verses: *philadelphia* – love of the brethren, an intimate, family word – as well as the more usual word for Christian love – *agapē*. The former stresses particularly love for their Christian brethren. Comparison with 3:12 might suggest they were good at that but were failing in love of their fellow-men, a probable state of affairs in view of their persecuted situation.

The rest of the exhortation (11,12) is concerned with practical details of living in pagan surroundings. From 5:14 and 2 Thess. 3:6-12 it is clear that some, excited by the prospect of Christ's return, were being lazy and had stopped working. So Paul tells them to have a threefold ambition: to live quietly, to do their own business and to work. They should live a normal, working life. 'With your hands' (11) could be an added comment not to despise manual labour – a typical Greek attitude. Once again Paul's commands have a clear purpose. The Thessalonians should give no reason, other than that of the gospel itself, for people to treat them with disrespect. Neither should they live off other people because of their own unwillingness to work.

THOUGHT: Our prayers need always to be appropriately followed up in active Christian work which in turn needs to be supported by prayer.

Questions for further study and discussion on 1 Thessalonians 2:17–4:12

1. Satan's job is to put stumbling blocks in our way (2:18). Our job is to turn them into stepping stones. How had Paul thwarted Satan? Have you any similar experiences?

2. Of 2:19 William Barclay says, 'At the last the stars in a man's crown will be those he has led nearer to Christ'. Do you think this applies to everyone? Is there anything more you can be doing individually or as a group, if so, what?

3. Paul is writing in deep distress, maybe because of difficulties in Athens and Corinth (3:7). What kept him going? Is there anyone you know whom you could encourage in some way?

4. 'If our faith causes us no suffering, perhaps we are not really working it out in our daily community life' (page 104). Do you agree with this? In what ways can Christianity bring persecution into our everyday lives?

5. What does Paul pray for in 3:11-13? What does this teach us about prayer?

6. Young Christians sometimes find it difficult to withstand the teaching of the 'new morality': sex before marriage is acceptable where there is love; divorce is acceptable where there is no love. How would you answer someone who genuinely believes this? See 4:3-8.

7. How does God teach us to love one another (4:9)? What do you think an increasing love would mean for you in practical terms?

8. In 4:11 Paul says, 'Don't be a lazy busybody.' Why not? When is it right to 'bear one another's burdens'? What is the difference?

4:13-18 The Christian hope

Chapter 4:13–5:11 deals with the specific problems raised by their understanding of and attitude to the second coming. Two specific problems appear to have been raised by the Thessalonians: the timing of the second coming (5:1-3) and the question of the state or fate of those Christians who die before the Lord comes. So Paul, with a favourite introduction – 'we would not have you ignorant, brethren' (13) – now addresses himself to this latter problem. It was an inevitable question in an age which expected the return of Christ in a matter of years, if not months.

Paul begins by referring to those who are dead as 'those who are sleeping'; so did Jesus in the case of Jairus' daughter (Luke 8:52). It is not an unknown description in Jewish and pagan writing but is an especially appropriate term for Christians. It should not, however, be forced into a basis for a theology of the state between death and the parousia. The New Testament is deliberately ambiguous in the matter; we should therefore take the hint and avoid speculation. Christian hope is based on what will happen at the return of Christ, not on some intermediate state. Christians need not grieve at death because we have a sure hope. This is based, first, on the fact of Christ's resurrection (14, compare 1 Cor. 15:12-22). By incorporation into Christ, his resurrection means ours. This seems to be the best way to understand the floating phrase 'through Jesus'. Secondly, it stems from the teaching of Jesus, though whether Paul by 'the word of the Lord' means a specific piece of Jesus' teaching or his own inspired understanding (compare 1 Cor. 7:10,25) is not clear. Its content is simply that those who have died will not be left behind when Christ appears. Rather they will be raised to life first, and then those who are still alive will join them and together they will go to be with Christ (16,17). The details are deliberately vague, both of the triumphant return of Christ (16) and what will happen afterwards. We are not meant to speculate or to try from this and other passages to construct some elaborate sequence of events. The source of comfort (18) is the resurrection of Christ, the certainty of Christ's return and the assurance that all in Christ, whether dead or alive, will rise, to be with him – 'so we shall always be with the Lord'. Paul's intention is to provide them with that secure basis, not to give precise details of a future event.

5:1-11 Sons of the day

Concerning the time of Jesus' second coming, Paul gives them the gentlest of rebukes: you know already that it will come like a thief in the night (compare Matt. 24:43). It had obviously formed part of his basic teaching on the Lord's return. All he will say is that Jesus' coming will shatter the complacency and security of the world outside the church, bringing ruin and loss. No one will escape. Everyone will then know his hour has come, just as a pregnant woman feels the onset of contractions and knows her labour has started.

In contrast to the surprise which the world will have, the Thessalonians should not be caught unawares. They are 'sons of light and sons of the day' (5). Both titles stress the fact that Christian characteristics are distinctive. In a world of darkness Christians are light; in a world of sleep and complacency they await the coming day. They must therefore live accordingly: 'be prepared' for his coming, both mentally – 'watch' – and morally – 'be sober' (6). The opposite conduct is characteristic of darkness. If we would prefer our actions and thoughts to be kept dark, it is often the case that we are not behaving as children of the day.

But what does it mean to be prepared for the return of Christ, to be children of the day? Once again the great Christian triad comes into its own. It means putting on the armour of faith, love and hope (8). The fact that Paul applies different qualities to the pieces of armour in Eph. 6 should warn us against pushing the metaphor too far. These Christian virtues will be our protection when Christ returns, because in them is summed up the gospel itself – we are not destined for destruction (3), but for life and salvation through Jesus Christ (9,10). 'Therefore encourage one another . . .' (11). The thought of the coming of Christ is always accompanied by a present imperative in the New Testament. It is, therefore, never escapism, for it provides the impetus for good living, mutual encouragement and growth in the present. Christian hope is as far removed from 'pie in the sky when you die' as chalk is from cheese.

5:12-22 Church life

Paul and his companions round off their letter with a group of practical exhortations about living together as a church. The first (12,13) concerns the respect and love which should be accorded to their church leaders. They are first described as those who labour (*kopiaō* – again a word describing hard physical toil) among them, before they are called those 'who are over you in the Lord and admonish you'. The New Testament doctrine of the Christian ministry is that it is a ministry of service. Its authority is not one of force, nor primarily of status, but, like that of Christ himself, is earned by service, and an application of the truth. Ministers are to be respected and loved because of the vital task they have to perform. Whether the exhortation to be at peace is to be understood in this context is not clear – was there rivalry between the elders at Thessalonica? Perhaps it is simply a general exhortation like those that follow. -

The remainder of the passage contains fourteen short exhortations to the church. They can be conveniently grouped together into four sections. The first (14) deals with the work of ministry. All should be involved in correcting the idle, and in encouraging and supporting each other. Secondly, their dealings with each other should show mutual love and respect (15). Thirdly (16,17), joy, prayer and thanksgiving should characterise their lives. Fourthly (19-21), spiritual life is not to be quenched. They must not 'pour cold water on the Spirit's inspiration', nor despise 'a word from God'. It should nevertheless be tested – there is no unquestioning acceptance of claimed inspiration. What is found to be good is to be 'held on to', while what is evil is to be rejected. The criteria for assessment are not given, but from the rest of the Bible we know they concern consistency with God's revealed truth and declared character (for example Gal. 1:8; 1 John 4:1-3; John 14:21-24; 1 John 1:8). It would be possible to take this last couplet as a distinct pair urging a life of good conduct, but it seems more natural to follow the context.

These are the standards of church life. It is a healthy thing to assess the standing of our own church in their light.

THOUGHT: The New Testament doctrine of the Christian ministry is that it is a ministry of service. Its authority is not one of force, nor primarily of status but, like that of Christ himself, is earned by service, and an application of the truth.

5:23-28 The God of peace

The closing words of the epistle contain Paul's final prayer (23,24), his last instructions (25-27) and the characteristic affirmation (28).

His prayer uses his favourite title for God. He is the author of all spiritual and physical well-being. Paul's request is that the Thessalonians may be completely set apart for God, and picks up the thought of 4:3 as well as the theme of the second coming. The division of body, soul and spirit is not necessarily an assertion of a tripartite nature in man. Rather it expresses the totality of his personality. Paul prays that their whole being may be kept pure and holy for the coming of Christ (compare 3:13).

The three brief requests reminded the Thessalonians first that Paul, Silas and Timothy also need their prayers. How often do we pray for those who pray for us? The second request might seem somewhat strange today, but the reference is found elsewhere in Paul's writing (Rom. 16:16; 1 Cor. 16:20; 2 Cor. 13:12). Fortunately we are learning the value of being more demonstrative in showing our love and affection for each other. The third request is surprisingly strong – 'I put you on oath to . . .'. Perhaps it is born out of Paul's strong desire to see the church again (so L. Morris) or maybe the dangers of a division in the church were greater than the letter implies.

The final affirmation typically (compare Phil. 4:23; Rom. 16:20) contains no verb. It is an assertion of the Christian gospel. The grace of our Lord Jesus Christ is with you.

Questions for further study and discussion on 1 Thessalonians 4:13–5:28

1. Amid all the speculations, what do we know for certain about the end of the world (4:13–5:11)? What are our fears and anxieties for the future? How can they be faced in Christ?

2. The second coming was evidently part of Paul's basic teaching. Why do you think it is so often neglected today? In what way do we suffer as a result?

3. The New Testament teaching is that Christ could return tomorrow. How can we be prepared for his coming (5:2-11)?

4. Paul saw that there were many faults in the Thessalonian church. Yet he begins his letter with unmixed praise before going on with his warnings. What harm do we do when we (a) concentrate just on someone's faults, (b) concentrate just on their good points?

5. It is all too easy to criticise our bosses and leaders (5:12,13). Why do you think this is? Do these verses mean that we should always support those over us?

6. J. B. Lightfoot has said, 'Thanksgiving is the end of all human conduct, whether observed in words or works' (5:16,18). Discuss your blessings and reasons for thanksgiving, and praise God for them.

7. Chapter 5:12-22 contains a list of characteristics of the Christian community. Which do you find most difficult to practise? How could your church life be improved?

1:1-4 Growing in adversity

The circumstances surrounding this second letter are not clear. Unlike its predecessor there is no historical section to help us (compare 1 Thess. 3.1-6). Little seems to have changed in the church since the first letter and the main themes concern similar problems: the return of Jesus Christ (2:1-12) and the indolence of church members (3:6-15). Perhaps William Barclay is right in suggesting that the Thessalonians had sent a letter or message which was full of self-doubt and Paul writes to encourage them. There is, however, no external evidence for the suggestion.

The opening verses are the same as those of 1 Thessalonians, with two minor alterations: the introduction of 'our' before Father in verse 1 and the addition of 'from God the Father and the Lord Jesus Christ'. This latter form of greeting occurs in almost all Paul's other epistles, reminding his readers that their source of grace and peace is God himself.

Again Paul begins with thanksgiving for their growing faith and increasing love, both of which he desired to see (1 Thess. 3:10, 12,13). The added note is that of boasting. In the first letter others boasted to Paul (1:8); now he boasts of them (4). He and his companions are spreading abroad the account of how the Thessalonians have stood firm under persecution and affliction. If we follow William Barclay's reconstruction of events, such comments are designed to remove their self-doubt and despair. Certainly Paul wishes to encourage them in their stand against persecution and rebuke.

1:5-10 The judgement of God

One of the questions uppermost in the minds of the Thessalonians must have concerned the reason for their affliction. Why did they have to suffer when those who persecuted the church apparently flourished? Paul's answer is to point to the righteousness of God and the reversal to be occasioned by his final judgement.

The opening verse (5) is not easy to unravel. It is not clear whether 'the evidence' refers to their steadfastness or their affliction. It seems to make better sense if we take it as referring to the former. 'Such constancy and faith . . . is clear evidence that God does not intend them to fall short of the final attainment of the kingdom' (L. Morris). In the context of verses 6-10 the phrase 'righteous judgement' (5) suggests 'the law of compensation by which the sufferers of this world shall rest hereafter and the persecutors of this world shall suffer hereafter' (R. H. Lightfoot). The coming of Christ will mean a great reversal.

On the one hand, those 'who do not know God' and 'who do not obey the gospel of our Lord Jesus will suffer punishment and exclusion from the presence of God. The thought of Christ 'inflicting vengeance' (8), even though it could better be translated 'giving punishment or retribution', is not an easy one to reconcile with the loving forgiveness of the man of Nazareth. We will, however, never fully understand the greatness of God's love until we set it against his justice and judgement. The gospel is not one of easy forgiveness, for sin must reap its reward. So the one who took a whip to purify the temple (John 2:15-17) will come in judgement to execute the justice of God as well as his love and mercy.

On the other hand Christ will be 'glorified in his saints' (10); he will be revealed as he really is, and will grant them rest from their afflictions (7).

THOUGHT: 'Here we have the breathtaking truth that our glory is Christ and that Christ's glory is ourselves. The glory of Christ is in those who through him have learned to endure and to suffer and to conquer, to shine like lights in a dark place, to become radiant with goodness and loveliness' (William Barclay).

1:11,12 Worthy of God's call

With God's judgement in mind Paul once again turns to prayer. He has already said that the Thessalonians' persecution makes them worthy of the kingdom of God (5). Now, having described their glorious future, he prays that God will make them worthy of the glory to which they are called. It is not a request to remove them from the fires of persecution but to refine them and fulfil their good resolves and their work of faith. The co-operation between God and man in the Christian life is strikingly displayed in this prayer. Our resolve and our faith are brought to fruition by God so that he may make us worthy of his calling.

Paul's second request gives the purpose of the first; 'so that the name of the Lord Jesus may be glorified in you'. That is a Hebraic way of saying, 'that the full character of Jesus Christ may be revealed in you'. The 'name' stood for the whole personality. 'Glorify' meant 'to reveal the full character'. Thus Christ is glorified as our lives manifest his character as we live 'in him'. The only way that this can be achieved is through a very close union with him. Such was Jesus' own prayer in John 17:1,10,21-23. It is a union which is only possible through or by the grace of our God and the Lord Jesus Christ. All this stems from the free and undeserved gift of God in Christ, but grace does not end with the process of conversion. Throughout our lives we need the grace of God so that the character of Christ may be worked out in our minds and bodies, in our total personality.

2:1,2 The coming of Christ

The letter now continues with its central theme – 'the coming of our Lord Jesus Christ'. Paul has already referred, in 1 Thess. 4:13-18 to his coming and their 'assembling to meet him'. It had been suggested the Lord had already come. Indeed, there even seems to have been a bogus letter from Paul to this effect (2). If such a letter existed, then it would account for the despondency of the Thessalonians – they had been left behind! – and the necessity of a second, genuine, letter from Paul authenticated in his own hand (3:17).

Paul urges them not to be easily tossed about by such reports. 'Do not suddenly lose your heads or alarm yourselves' (NEB). The Greek phrase stresses the importance of the mind: if their thinking is wrong on the subject then they will be thrown off course. Even if some prophetic utterance (compare 1 Thess. 5:20,21) is given, or 'a word', probably some kind of official pronouncement (GNB, 'prophesying or preaching') or a letter saying the day of the Lord has come, they must not get into a panic.

Sections of the church often display too much interest in looking for signs of the end. The history of such movements only serves to underline the wisdom of Paul's words. The Montanists, for example, ended up in the desert, expecting an end which never came. Church history is littered with similar groups. More subtle, and therefore more dangerous, are books claiming to interpret all the signs of the Bible in terms of present or future world phenomena, like Hal Lindsay's *The Late Great Planet Earth*. Such books must be carefully judged by the Bible itself, and the overwhelming opinion and interpretation of scholars down the church's history. We must not allow what R. T. France has called 'the papacy of the popular paperback' to upset our thinking too easily, or we are falling into the same trap as the Thessalonians.

2:3-12 The man of lawlessness

If we are to understand this difficult passage aright, it is important that Paul's purpose in writing is kept in view. He is trying to remind the Thessalonians of his basic teaching about the coming of Christ so that they will not be quickly blown off course by a spurious claim that Christ has already come. It is in this context that Paul speaks of 'the rebellion' and the 'revealing of the man of lawlessness'. Both these events will precede the coming of Christ.

In these descriptions Paul is drawing on both Old Testament imagery (see, e.g., Dan. 7:24,25; 8:9-12; 11:36-39) and the contemporary Jewish understanding of the climax of history. For example 'the mystery of lawlessness' (7), which is said to be already at work, is a phrase which turns up in the Qumran manuscripts (the 'Dead Sea Scrolls'). It obviously meant something then of which we are no longer aware today, and is parallel to the idea of the Antichrist (compare 1 John 2:18, 22-23; 4:3; 2 John 7). Paul's readers would obviously understand it in the light of these ideas and some of the allusions would be clearer to them than to us (compare verse 6). Leaving the details on one side, Paul argues that Christ could not already have returned, for 'the rebellion' had not taken place, and 'the man of lawlessness' was still being restrained (3,6,7). Adding all the clues together, it appears that Paul envisages a period before the coming of Christ of unparalleled opposition to him. It is to be led by a force of evil in the world whose aim will be to oppose and replace every form of religion and worship (4). Whether this 'man of lawlessness' is to be interpreted as an individual, a corporate organisation or an ideology is not clear (see additional note below). For the moment his activity is being restrained (6,7) although he is already at work. The restraining force is better understood in terms of the principle of law and order (L. Morris) than as a reference to the Roman Empire (William Barclay). In the latter case the problem of identity is acute, for v.8 implies that the man of lawlessness will be openly seen with the collapse of the restraint. No obvious candidate arose when Rome fell.

From this difficult passage three clear strands emerge. First, there is a force of evil at work in the world whose inspiration is Satanic (9) and whose methods are deceit, delusion and unrighteousness. Such a force will not grow less but rather increase throughout history. Secondly, in spite of appearances to the contrary, God is in control even of the evil itself (11,12). Thirdly, the ultimate victory will be that of Christ himself (8) at his coming.

Additional note on eschatology and 'the man of lawlessness'

Ten years ago it was fashionable to interpret eschatology, the doctrine of the last things, in terms of one of three theories. There was C. H. Dodd's theory of 'realised eschatology'. This stressed the fact that in Jesus the kingdom of God had come (had been 'realised'), and interpreted the eschatological elements of the New Testament by making them apply to the New Testament era. Such an approach provides many valuable insights but it cannot really satisfy the strong element of future fulfilment which runs throughout the New Testament, a fact which Dodd himself acknowledged. More radically R. Bultmann suggested that all these passages were 'myths' in the specialised sense of a story which has present existential significance. Whether or not the story is true is not relevant to its meaning. Eschatology therefore becomes a way of talking about present history in terms of Jewish ideas of apocalyptic and of gnostic ideas which belong to a pre-scientific age. Finally, O. Cullmann provided a more orthodox understanding by seeing the 'Christ-event' as the mid-point of salvation history. Eschatology deals with all the events from the incarnation to the parousia. If Christ's death and resurrection was 'the decisive battle' of the war, his return would be his 'Victory Day'.

In more recent years, W. Pannenberg and J. Moltmann have stressed that we can only understand history and Christ in terms of their completion, so that both receive their unity and meaning from the goal of all things. Eschatology then becomes, not the appendix to Christian doctrine, but the goal which gives everything else its meaning.

The strange, variously described, figure that strides across the New Testament must be understood within the context of our general interpretation of eschatology. The 'abomination of desolation' (Mark 13), 'the man of lawlessness' (2 Thess. 2), the antichrists (1 John) and the beasts (Rev. 13) have been interpreted in terms of historical persons, ranging from Nero to a supposed son of the American Ambassador (in the film *The Omen*), or of ideologies like Communism, or as a more general expression of antichristian thought, whatever and however it is expressed. Its meaning was presumably clear to Paul's readers but it is a meaning which has vanished in the mists of history. Perhaps the most satisfactory solution to the problem is to follow the illuminating framework suggested by Pannenberg and Moltmann. If the goal of history is the establishment of God's kingdom and the universal rule of Christ, of which the cross and resurrection is the present promise, then the establishment of that universal rule must be preceded by the final defeat *in history* of the forces of evil which oppose it. This is the overthrow of 'the man of lawlessness'. The restraint might then refer to the structures of civilisation which make the present coexistence of good and evil possible. The decisive conflict will come, perhaps continually comes, as and when such structures are destroyed.

Questions for further study and discussion on 2 Thessalonians 1:1–2:12

1. How did persecution strengthen the Thessalonian church (1:3-5)? In your experience how has suffering or trouble strengthened your life or the life of your church?

2. How did Paul encourage the downcast Thessalonians? The ability to encourage is a gift from God. What qualities would you say are needed?

3. What do 1:7-10 and 2:1-9 teach about (a) the strength of Satan, (b) the power of Jesus Christ? What do you find most challenging and encouraging about this?

4. There are some modern speculations about what happens at death (for example the interest in people who apparently die, meet a 'figure of light' and are sent back to this world). What principles can we apply when people discuss these with us (compare note on 1:5-10)?

5. How far is your present Christian experience influenced by what we call 'eschatology' – the understanding of the last things: death, judgement, the return of Christ? In the light of these chapters should it have more or less influence?

6. What fears and questions do you have about life after death, heaven, the last judgement? How can we face our fears and questions in Christ?

7. Look up all the passages referring to the Antichrist and similar ideas. With the help of commentaries, where necessary, try to assess the significance of this figure. How far do you agree with the approach outlined above?

2:13-15 The divine initiative

In contrast to those 'who did not believe the truth but had pleasure in unrighteousness' (12), Paul thinks of the faith and obedience of the Thessalonians. He reminds his readers of the obligation which is laid on him and his companions to thank God for them. The obligation is there because of God's choice and their response. In two short sentences (13,14) he outlines the gospel itself.

The gospel begins with the choice and call of God. There is a subtle temptation to imagine that we are the prime movers in our salvation but this is a delusion. God is complete in himself and does not need our love, yet of his own will he chose us and called us in the gospel to enter a new and intimate relationship with himself. The phrase 'from the beginning' is not just implying that God exercised his choice a long time ago but is an echo of the Pauline assertion that the whole purpose of creation was to create a kingdom of redeemed humanity. You cannot make sense of creation except in the light of God's new creation – the coming kingdom of God (compare Ephesians 1). The process by which this is achieved is the double one of 'sanctification by the Spirit and belief in the truth' (13). We rightly think of sanctification as the process of making us more like Christ. It essentially means the complete setting apart of a man for God. As such it is both an initial action and a continuous refinement. By the Spirit we have been marked out as God's men. By the same Spirit this is a growing reality in our lives. We are not mere puppets, however, for the response to God's initiative is the belief in the truth. The purpose of it all is that we may obtain the glory of Jesus Christ himself (compare 1:12). If that end is to be achieved the Thessalonians must stand firm and be faithful to what they have been taught (15). As Christians our final assurance is the ability to stay the course and hold firm to our beliefs and experience of the Spirit.

2:16,17 The God of love and comfort

The main teaching section of the letter is brought to an end with prayer (compare 1 Thess. 3:11-13). Paul prays to the Lord Jesus Christ and to the Father who he describes as the one who has loved us (*agapaō*) and has given us eternal comfort (*paraklēsis*) and good hope through grace. These probably refer to God's love in sending his Son, and his gift of the Spirit as a constant source of strength. The word *paraklēsis* is from the same root as *paraklētos*, which is used as a title for the Spirit in John's Gospel. Although the Gospel is certainly later in date than this epistle, Paul would have been familiar with the title. The Spirit is our source of strength and encouragement. The second gift of grace is good hope, good both in the sense that it is genuine hope and also in its effects.

The substance of Paul's prayer arises from these gifts of grace. It is that God will comfort and strengthen the Thessalonians (*parakaleō*) in their hearts – the source of their will and emotions – and make them firm in deed and word. On this occasion Paul makes no parallel request for himself (compare 1 Thess. 3:11-13) that he might see them. Perhaps he had heard enough to reassure himself that they were sufficiently mature to stand firm.

3:1-5 A prayer request

The rather curt 'Brethren, pray for us' (compare 1 Thess. 5:25) is here expanded to include two specific requests. It was often Paul's custom to ask the support of the churches in prayer (for example compare Eph. 6:19; Col. 4:3). On almost every occasion his first request is for the preaching of the gospel. Once again he goes back to the Greek games for his metaphor as he prays that God's word may 'run and be glorified' elsewhere as it had at Thessalonica. Probably he is referring to its proclamation and its welcome reception. Secondly, he prays for his own safety (2). If Paul is writing from Corinth he is probably thinking of the Jews who had failed to receive his message and stirred up opposition against him (Acts 18:5,6,12).

Having made his simple requests, Paul turns once again to the Thessalonians. In contrast to those who have no faith – perhaps a reference to the constant refusal of the Jews to accept his message – God remains faithful. The force of the contrast is reduced in translation for in the Greek text the ending of the previous phrase in v.2 is *pistis*, faith, while v.3 begins *'pistos . . .'* – 'faithful is the Lord'. Men may not accept his message, but God will care for those who have done so – in this case the Thessalonians. It is for this reason that Paul is confident they will heed his instructions, provided their hearts continue to be centred on the love of God and the patience and steadfastness of Christ.

3:6-13 Idleness rebuked

'We command you . . .'. With exactly the same word as in v.4 Paul lays down his instruction which he is so sure they will heed. Perhaps because some have ignored his previous instruction (10), Paul is very firm in dealing with the persistent problem of idleness. The person who is to be shunned is literally the one who is disorderly. W. Barclay paraphrases it as 'truants from duty and from work'. Probably excited by the imminent prospect of the coming of Christ, they had given up work and not bothered with their duties at home and in church. Paul will have none of it and cites his own example (7-9). Although as evangelists he and his companions had the right to be looked after (compare 1 Thess. 2:6) they had not claimed this right but had laboured night and day, in order not to put a burden on the church. So those 'busybodies who are not doing any business' – there is a pun in the Greek – are told to work quietly and earn an honest living (12), 'eat their own bread'! In a largely agricultural society, the link between work and food was very close. If you failed to work the land, then the crops would fail you. Paul's words could therefore be paraphrased, 'Do not come to the rescue of the man who has no bread purely through his own deliberate fault.' Paul's words have, however, nothing to do with the situation which is all too common today where men, through no fault of their own, are unable to find work.

3:14-18 Community action

So deeply entrenched was the idleness at Thessalonica that Paul anticipates that some will not listen to his commands. He therefore repeats the order he has already given (6), that anyone who disobeys him is to be shunned. But Paul writes this with a clear purpose in view, 'that he may be ashamed'. To be 'sent to Coventry' is never pleasant and Paul only advocates it here in order to bring the wanderer back into the fold. Any vindictiveness is out. He must not be dealt with like an enemy. The action of avoiding him must not obscure the fact that he is a brother and he must be treated with brotherly love. Discipline is never easy within the church fellowship. It should be exercised corporately and with the purpose of restoration clearly in view. Loving rebuke is part of church life, vindictive judgement is not. Throughout the history of the church, excommunication has been exercised by both Catholic and Protestant churches as a means of purging the congregation. Paul's words suggest that it should rather be looked on as a means of restoring the wayward. If a ban of excommunication continues it has failed in its objective.

Once again Paul commends his readers to the God of peace (see on 1 Thess. 5:23), and adds his final blessing. Again it could be accurately translated as the Lord is with you all: a mark of Christian confidence rather than a prayer.

Perhaps with the spurious letter in mind (2:2) Paul adds a postscript in his own hand as a guarantee that he is the true author. He draws attention to this special greeting in his own hand in two other letters (see 1 Cor. 16:21 and Col. 4:18). Paul added a greeting on all his letters (17) though he doesn't elsewhere comment on it. To write the greeting at the end of a letter was a similar practice to our adding our signature. The greeting itself is the same as that of 1 Thess. 5:28 'the grace of our Lord Jesus Christ is with you all'.

Questions for further study and discussion on 2 Thessalonians 2:13–3:18

1. The Christian life begins with God's call (2:13). When in your own life have you been particularly aware of God's call? How did you know it was God?

2. In what ways do we or should we allow for the call of God in our evangelistic work? How clearly do we stress God's initiative?

3. O. Hallesby has written, 'To pray is to open the door to Jesus and to admit him in your distress.' What distress did Paul ask prayer for in 3:1-3? What was his confidence? How does that help us in similar situations?

4. Why did Paul speak so strictly against idleness (6-12)? Do you think this still applies today?

5. Today and in future years we are increasingly going to find ourselves in a situation 'where men, through no fault of their own, are unable to find work' (page 126). What problems will these people face? What should be the Christian approach in such situations?

6. What place has discipline in the life of the local church? How should it be exercised? How should 3:14 be applied?

7. What is the most important lesson you have learnt from Paul's letters to the Thessalonians?